P9-CMF-105

WHEATON COLLEGE LIBRARY
Norton, Massachusetts

English Men of Letters

EDITED BY JOHN MORLEY

BENTLEY

BY

R. C. JEBB, M.A., LL.D. Edin.

KNIGHT OF THE ORDER OF THE SAVIOUR
PROFESSOR OF GREEK IN THE UNIVERSITY OF GLASGOW
FORMERLY FELLOW OF TRINITY COLLEGE, CAMBRIDGE

NEW YORK

HARPER & BROTHERS, PUBLISHERS

FRANKLIN SQUARE

1882

PA
85
B4J4
1882

B

4687

PREFATORY NOTE.

THE following are the principal sources for an estimate of Bentley's life and work:

1. Life of Bentley, by J. H. Monk, 4to, London, 1830: 2nd ed., 2 vols. 8vo, 1833.—2. Bentley's Correspondence, ed. C. Wordsworth, 2 vols., Lond. 1842.—3. Bentley's Works, ed. Alex. Dyce, 1836–38. Vols. I. and II.—Dissertation on Letters of Phalaris, (1) as published in 1699, (2) as originally printed in Wotton's *Reflections*, 1697. Epistola ad Ioannem Millium. Vol. III.—Boyle Lectures, with Newton's Letters: Sermons: Remarks upon a late Discourse of Freethinking: Proposals for an edition of the New Testament: Answer to the Remarks of Conyers Middleton.—4. Bentley's Fragments of Callimachus, in the edition of Graevius, Utrecht, 1697, reprinted in Blomfield's ed., London, 1815.—5. Emendations on Menander and Philemon (1710), reprinted, Cambridge, 1713.—6. Horace, Camb. 1711, 2nd ed., Amsterdam, 1713.—7. Terence, Cambridge, 1726, 2nd ed., Amsterdam, 1728.—8. Milton's *Paradise Lost*, London, 1732. —9. Manilius, London, 1739.

Notes by Bentley appeared during his lifetime in the books of other scholars. Since his death, many more have been published from his MSS. These, while varying much in fulness and value, cannot be overlooked in a survey of the field which his studies covered. The subjoined list comprises the greater part of them:

On Cicero's Tusculan Disputations, in Gaisford's ed., Oxford, 1805. —Hephæstion, in Gaisford's ed., 1810.—Lucretius, in Oxford ed.,

1818.—Horace (curae novissimae), in the Cambridge Museum Criticum, I. 194–6, ed. T. Kidd.—Ovid, in the Classical Journal, XIX. 168, 258, ed. G Burges.—Lucan, ed. R. Cumberland, Strawberry Hill, 1760. —Silius Italicus, Class. Journ. III. 381.—L. Annæus Seneca, ib. XXXVII. 11, ed. T. Kidd.—Nicander, in Museum Criticum, I. 370, 445, ed. J. H. Monk.—Aristophanes, in Classical Journal, XI. 131, 248, XII. 104, 352, XIII. 132, 336, XIV. 130, ed. G. Burges; and in Museum Criticum, II. 126, ed. J. H. Monk.—Sophocles, Theocritus, Bion, Moschus, ed. E. Maltby in Morell's Thesaurus, reprinted in Classical Journal, XIII. 244.—Philostratus, in Olearius's edition (1709).—Hierocles, in Needham's edition (1709).—Plautus, in E. A. Sonnenschein's ed. of the Captivi, p. 135, Lond. 1880.—Iliad, I. II., at the end of J. Maehly's memoir of Bentley (1868), from the MS. at Trinity College, Cambridge.—Selected Notes on the Greek Testament (from the MS. at Trin. Coll., Camb.), including those on the Epistle to the Galatians, in *Bentleii Critica Sacra*, ed. A. A. Ellis, Camb. 1862.—A few anecdota from Bentley's MS. notes on Homer (at Trin. Coll., Camb.) are given on page 150.

R. Cumberland's *Memoirs* (4to, 1806, 2nd edition, in 2 vols. 8vo, 1807) deserve to be consulted independently of Monk's quotations from them. The memoir of Bentley by F. A. Wolf, in his *Litterarische Analekten* (pp. 1–89, Berlin, 1816), has the permanent interest of its authorship and its date. Rud's Diary, so useful for a part of Bentley's college history, was edited, with some additional letters, by H. R. Luard for the Cambridge Antiquarian Society, 1860. De Quincey's essay—originally a review of Monk—has every charm of his style; the sometimes whimsical judgments need not be taken too seriously. Hartley Coleridge's comments on Monk's facts may be seen in the short biography of Bentley which he wrote in the *Worthies of Yorkshire and Lancashire* (pp. 65–174). In " Richard Bentley, eine Biographie" (Leipzig, 1868), Jacob Maehly gives a concise sketch for German readers, on

Monk's plan of a continuous chronological narrative, in which notices of the literary works are inserted as they occur.

It is proper to state the points which are distinctive of the present volume: 1. In regard to the external facts of Bentley's life, I have been able to add some traits or illustrations from contemporary or other sources: these are chiefly in chapters I. III. VII. XII.— 2. Chapter VI. is condensed from some results of studies in the University life of Bentley's time, and in the history of Trinity College.—3. The controversy on the Letters of Phalaris has hitherto been most familiar to English readers through De Quincey's essay on Bentley, or the brilliant passage in Macaulay's essay on Temple. Both versions are based on Monk's. The account given here will be found to present some matters under a different light. In such cases the views are those to which I was led by a careful examination of the original sources, and of all the literary evidence which I could find.—4. My aim has been not more to sketch the facts of Bentley's life than to estimate his work, the character of his powers, and his place in scholarship. Here the fundamental materials are Bentley's writings themselves. To these I have given a comparatively large share of the allotted space. My treatment of them has been independent of any predecessor.

The courtesy of the Master of Trinity afforded me an opportunity of using Bentley's marginal notes on Homer at a time when they would not otherwise have been accessible. Mr. Tyrrell, Regius Professor of Greek in the University of Dublin, favoured me with information regarding a manuscript in the Library.

Prof. A. Michaelis, of Strassburg, and Mr. J. W. Clark, of Trinity College, Cambridge, kindly lent me some books and tracts relating to Bentley.

My thanks are especially due to Dr. Hort, for reading the proof-sheets of chapter x.; and to Mr. Munro, for reading those of chapters VIII. and IX. To both I have owed most valuable suggestions. For others, on many points, I have been indebted to Dr. Luard, Registrary of the University of Cambridge; who, with a kindness which I cannot adequately acknowledge, has done me the great favour of reading the whole book during its passage through the press.

THE COLLEGE, GLASGOW,
    February, 1882.

ANNALS OF BENTLEY'S LIFE.

	Æt.	I. EARLIER PERIOD.—1662-1699.
1662		Jan. 27. Birth.
1672	10	Goes to Wakefield School.
1676	14	Enters St. John's Coll., Cambridge.
1680	18	B.A. Degree.
1682	20	Master of Spalding School. Tutor to J. Stillingfleet.
1683	21	M.A. Degree.
1685	23	**James II.**
1689	27	**William and Mary.** Goes with J. Stillingfleet to Oxford.
1690	28	Ordained. Chaplain to Bp. Stillingfleet.
1691	29	*Letter to Mill.*
1692	30	*Boyle Lectures.* Prebendary of Worcester. Temple's *Essay.*
1693	31	*Fragments of Callimachus.* Nominated King's Librarian.
1694	32	Appointed, April 12. Wotton's *Reflections.*
1695	33	Chaplain in Ordinary to King.—F.R.S.—Boyle's *Phalaris.*
1696	34	Promotes reparation of Camb. Press.—D.D.
1697	35	First essay on Phalaris in 2nd ed. of Wotton.
1698	36	Jan. "*Boyle against Bentley.*"
1699	37	Mar. "*Bentley against Boyle.*"—Master of Trin. Coll., Camb.
		II. AT CAMBRIDGE.—1700-1742.
1700	38	Feb. 1. Installed at Trin.—Vice-Chancellor.
1701	39	Jan. 7. Marriage.—Archdeacon of Ely.

	Æt.	
1702	40	**Anne.**
1702–4	40–2	College Reforms.—Swift's *Battle of the Books* (**1704**).
1706–8	44–6	Aids L. Küster, T. Hemsterhuys.
1710	48	Feb. 10. Petition from Fellows of Trin. to Bp. Moore. *Menander and Philemon.*—Thornhill's portrait of B.
1711	49	Dec. 8. *Horace.*
1713	51	Bp. cites B. to Ely House. *Remarks* in reply to Collins.
1714	52	FIRST TRIAL AT ELY HOUSE.—July 31. Bp. Moore dies before judgment has been given. Aug. 1. Death of Queen Anne. **George I.**
1715	53	Jacobite Revolt. B.'s *Sermon on Popery.*
1716	54	Petition from Fellows of Trin. to Crown.
1717	55	B. Regius Prof. of Divinity. George I. visits Cambridge.
1718	56	B. arrested. Deprived of Degrees by Senate (Oct. 17).
1719	57	B. makes terms with Miller.
1720	58	*Proposals* for edition of New Testament.
1724	62	Mar. 26. B.'s degrees restored.—Declines see of Bristol.
1725	63	B.'s Latin speech at Commencement.
1726	64	*Terence* published.
1727	65	**George II.** Death of Newton.
1728	66	George II. at Cambridge.—B.'s illness.—Colbatch active.
1729	67	Bp. Greene cites B. to appear. Veto by King's Bench.
1730	68	Senate House opened.
1731	69	Fire at Cottonian Library.
1732	70	B.'s edition of *Paradise Lost.* He undertakes Homer.
1733	71	SECOND TRIAL AT ELY HOUSE.
1734	72	April 27. Bp. Greene sentences B. to deprivation.
1735–7	73–5	Efforts to procure execution of the judgment.
1738	76	April 22. End of the struggle. B. remains in possession.
1739	77	*Manilius.*
1740	78	Death of Mrs. Bentley.
1742	80	March. Pope's enlarged *Dunciad*, with verses on B. June. B. examines for the Craven. July 14. His death.

DATES OF SOME PRINCIPAL WORKS.

1691	29	Letter to Mill.
1692	30	Boyle Lectures.
1693	31	Fragments of Callimachus.
1699	37	Enlarged Dissertation on Phalaris.
1710	48	Emendations on Menander and Philemon.
1711	49	Horace.
1713	51	Remarks on a late Discourse of Free-thinking.
1726	64	Terence.
1732	70	Edition of *Paradise Lost.*
1739	77	Manilius.

1*

CONTENTS.

BENTLEY.

CHAPTER I.

EARLY LIFE.—THE LETTER TO MILL.

RICHARD BENTLEY was born on January 27, 1662. A remarkable variety of interest belongs to his life of eighty years. He is the classical critic whose thoroughly original genius set a new example of method, and gave a decisive bent to the subsequent course of scholarship. Amongst students of the Greek Testament he is memorable as the first who defined a plan for constructing the whole text directly from the oldest documents. His English style has a place of its own in the transition from the prose of the seventeenth century to that of the eighteenth. During forty years he was the most prominent figure of a great English University at a stirring period. And everything that he did or wrote bears a vivid impress of personal character. The character may alternately attract and repel; it may provoke a feeling in which indignation is tempered only by a sense of the ludicrous, or it may irresistibly appeal to our admiration; but at all moments and in all moods it is signally masterful.

His birthplace was Oulton, a township in the parish of Rothwell, near Wakefield, in the West Riding of Yorkshire. His family were yeomen of the richer class, who for some generations had held property in the neighbourhood of Halifax. Bentley's grandfather had been a captain in the Royalist army during the civil war, and had died whilst a prisoner in the hands of the enemy. The Bentleys suffered in fortune for their attachment to the Cavalier party, but Thomas Bentley, Richard's father, still owned a small estate at Woodlesford, a village in the same parish as Oulton. After the death of his first wife, Thomas Bentley, then an elderly man, married in 1661 Sarah, daughter of Richard Willie, of Oulton, who is described as a stone-mason, but seems to have been rather what would now be called a builder, and must have been in pretty good circumstances; he is said to have held a major's commission in the royal army during the troubles. It was after him that his daughter's first-born was called Richard. Bentley's literary assailants in later years endeavoured to represent him as a sort of ploughboy who had been developed into a learned boor; whilst his amiable and accomplished grandson, Richard Cumberland, exhibited a pardonable tendency to over-estimate the family claims. Bentley himself appears to have said nothing on the subject.

He was taught Latin grammar by his mother. From a day-school at Methley, a village near Oulton, he was sent to the Wakefield Grammar School—probably when he was not more than eleven years old, as he went to Cambridge at fourteen. School-boy life must have been more cheerful after the Restoration than it had been before, to judge from that lively picture in North's "Lives" of the school at Bury St. Edmund's, where the master—a staunch Royalist—was forced, " in the dregs of time," to observe " super-hypocritical fastings and seekings," and " walked to church after his brigade of boys, there to endure the infliction of divers holdersforth." Then the King came to his own again, and this scholastic martyr had the happy idea of "publishing his cavaliership by putting all the boys at his school into red cloaks;" "of whom he had near thirty to parade before him, through that observing town, to church; which made no vulgar appearance." The only notice of Bentley's school-life by himself (so far as I know) is in Cumberland's *Memoirs*, and is highly characteristic. "I have had from him at times whilst standing at his elbow "—says his grandson, who was then a boy about nine years old—" a complete and entertaining narrative of his school-boy days, with the characters of his different masters very humorously displayed, and the punishments described which they at times would wrongfully inflict upon him for seeming to be idle and regardless of his task—*When the dunces*, he would say, *could not discover that I was pondering it in my mind, and fixing it more firmly in my memory, than if I had been bawling it out amongst the rest of my school-fellows.*" However, he seems to have retained through life a warm regard for Wakefield School. It had a high reputation. Another of its pupils, a few years later, was John Potter, author of the once popular work on Greek antiquities, editor of Lycophron, and afterwards Archbishop of Canterbury.

Bentley was only thirteen when his father died. His grandfather, Richard Willie, decided that he should go to the University without much more delay. The boy had his own way to make; his father's small estate had been left to a son by the first marriage; and in those days there was nothing to hinder a precocious lad from matriculating at fourteen, though the ordinary age was already seventeen or eighteen. On May 24, 1676, "Ricardus Bentley de Oulton" was enrolled in the Admission Book of St. John's College. The choice of a University may have been influenced by the fact that John Baskervile, the master of Wakefield School, was a member of Emmanuel College, Cambridge; the choice of a College, partly by the fact that some scholarships for natives of Yorkshire had been founded at St. John's by Sir Marmaduke Constable. Bentley, like Isaac Newton at Trinity, entered as a subsizar, a student who receives certain allowances. St. John's College was just then the largest in the University, and appears to have been as efficient as it was distinguished. The only relic of Bentley's undergraduate life is a copy of English verses on the Gunpowder Plot. That stirring theme was long a stock subject for College exercises. Bentley's verses have the jerky vigour of a youth whose head is full of classical allusions, and who is bent on making points. The social life of the University probably did not engage very much of his time; and it is left to us to conjecture how much he saw of two Cambridge contemporaries who afterwards wrote against him—Richard Johnson, of his own College, and Garth, the poet, of Peterhouse; or of William Wotton, his firm friend in later life —that "juvenile prodigy" who was a boy of fourteen when Bentley took his degree, and yet already a Bachelor of Arts.

Nothing is known of Bentley's classical studies whilst he was an undergraduate. His own statement, that some of his views on metrical questions dated from earliest manhood (*iam ab adolescentia*), is too vague to prove anything. Monk remarks that there were no prizes for classics at Cambridge then. It may be observed, however, that there was one very important prize—the Craven University Scholarship, founded in 1647. But no competition is recorded between 1670, when Bentley was eight years old, and 1681, the year after he took his first degree. The studies of the Cambridge Schools were Logic, Ethics, Natural Philosophy, and Mathematics. Bentley took high honours in these. His place was nominally sixth in the first class, but really third, since three of those above him were men of straw. The Vice-chancellor and the two Proctors then possessed the privilege of interpolating one name each in the list, simply as a compliment, and they naturally felt that such a compliment was nothing if it was not courageous. Bentley's degree had no real likeness, of course, to that of third Wrangler now; modern Mathematics were only beginning, and the other subjects of the Schools had more weight; the testing process, too, was far from thorough.

Bentley never got a Fellowship. In his time—indeed, until the present century—there were territorial restrictions at almost all Colleges. As a native of Yorkshire, he had been elected to a Constable scholarship, but the same circumstance excluded him from a greater prize. When he graduated, two Fellowships at St. John's were already held by Yorkshiremen, and a third representative of the same county was inadmissible. He was a candidate, indeed, in 1682; but as no person not in Priest's Orders was eligible on that occasion, he must have gone in merely to show what he could do. The College was enabled to recognise him in other ways, however. He was appointed to the mastership of Spalding School in Lincolnshire. At the end of about a year, he quitted this post for one which offered attractions of a different kind. Dr. Stillingfleet—then Dean of St. Paul's, and formerly a

Fellow of St. John's, Cambridge—wanted a tutor for his second son : and his choice fell on Bentley.

A youth of twenty-one, with Bentley's tastes and powers, could scarcely have been placed in a more advantageous position. Stillingfleet was already foremost amongst those scholarly divines who were regarded as the champions of Christianity against deists or materialists, and more particularly as defenders of the English Church against designs which had been believed to menace it since the Restoration. The researches embodied in Stillingfleet's *Origines Sacrae* and other works had for their general aim to place the Anglican religion on the historical basis of primitive times. In the course of his extensive and varied studies, he had gradually formed that noble library—one of the finest private collections then existing in England—which after his death was purchased for Dublin by Archbishop Marsh. Free access to such a library was a priceless boon for Bentley. At the Dean's house he would also meet the best literary society in London ; and his " patron "—to use the phrase of that day—received him on a footing which enabled him to profit fully by such opportunities. Stillingfleet could sympathise with the studies of his son's young tutor. In his own early days, after taking his degree at the same College, Stillingfleet had accepted a domestic tutorship, and " besides his attendance on his proper province, the instruction of the young gentleman," had found time to set about writing his *Irenicum*—the endeavour of a sanguine youth to make peace between Presbyterians and Prelacy. A contemporary biographer (Dr. Timothy Goodwin) has thus described Dr. Stillingfleet: " He was tall, graceful, and well-proportioned ; his countenance comely, fresh, and awful ; in his conversation, cheerful and discreet, obliging, and very instructive." To the day of

his death in 1699 Stillingfleet was Bentley's best friend—
the architect, indeed, of his early fortunes.

The next six years, from the twenty-first to the twenty-
seventh of his age (1683–1689), were passed by Bentley
in Dr. Stillingfleet's family. It was during this period,
when he enjoyed much leisure and the use of a first-rate
library, that Bentley laid the solid foundations of his
learning. He enlarged his study of the Greek and Latin
classics, writing notes in the margin of his books as he
went along. In those days, it will be remembered, such
studies were not facilitated by copious dictionaries of
classical biography, geography, and antiquities, or by those
well-ordered and comprehensive lexicons which exhibit at
a glance the results attained by the labours of successive
generations. Bentley now began to make for himself lists
of the authors whom he found cited by the ancient grammarians; and it may be observed that a series of detractors, from Boyle's allies to Richard Dawes, constantly twit
Bentley with owing all his learning to "indexes." Thus,
in a copy of verses preserved by Granger, Bentley figures as

> "Zoilus, tir'd with turning o'er
> Dull indexes, a precious store."

At this time he also studied the New Testament critically.
His labours on the Old Testament may be described in his
own words: "I wrote, before I was twenty-four years of
age, a sort of *Hexapla;* a thick volume in quarto, in the
first column of which I inserted every word of the Hebrew
Bible alphabetically; and, in five other columns, all the
various interpretations of those words in the Chaldee, Syriac, Vulgate, Latin, Septuagint, and Aquila, Symmachus,
and Theodotion, that occur in the whole Bible."

Bentley did not take Orders till 1690, when he was

twenty-eight, but he had probably always intended to do so. His delay may have been partly due to the troubles of James II.'s reign. Immediately after the Revolution Dean Stillingfleet was raised to the see of Worcester. His eldest son had gone to Cambridge; but Bentley's pupil, James, was sent to Wadham College, Oxford. Bentley accompanied him thither; and, having taken an *ad eundem* degree of M.A., was placed on the books of Wadham College. He continued to reside at Oxford till the latter part of 1690; and we find him engaged on be-half of the University in negotiations for the purchase of the library which had belonged to Dr. Isaac Voss, Canon of Windsor. This valuable collection—including the books of Gerard John Voss, Isaac's father—ultimate-ly went to Leyden; not, apparently, through any fault of Bentley's, though that was alleged during his controversy with Boyle.

While living at Oxford, Bentley enjoyed access to the Bodleian Library; and, as if his ardour had been stimu-lated by a survey of its treasures, it is at this time that his literary projects first come into view. "I had de-cided" (he informs Dr. Mill) "to edit the fragments of all the Greek poets, with emendations and notes, as a sin-gle great work." Perhaps even Bentley can scarcely then have realised the whole magnitude of such a task, and would have gauged it more accurately two years later, when he had edited the fragments of Callimachus. Nor was this the only vast scheme that floated before his mind. In a letter to Dr. Edward Bernard (then Savilian Professor of Astronomy at Oxford) he discloses a project of editing three Greek lexicons—those of Hesychius and Suidas, with the *Etymologicum Magnum*—in three paral-lel columns for each page. These would make three folio

volumes; a fourth volume would contain other lexicons
(as those of Julius Pollux, Erotian, and Phrynichus) which
did not lend themselves to the arrangement in column.
His thoughts were also busy with Philostratus (the Greek
biographer of the Sophists)—with Lucretius—and with
the astronomical poet Manilius.   Bentley excelled all previous scholars in accurate knowledge of the classical metres.   His sojourn at Oxford is the earliest moment at
which we find a definite notice of his metrical studies.
The Baroccian collection in the Bodleian Library contains
some manuscripts of the Greek "Hand-book of Metres"
which has come down under the name of the grammarian
Hephaestion.   Bentley now collated these, using a copy
of the edition of Turnebus, in which he made some marginal notes; the book is in the Library of Trinity College,
Cambridge.

When Bentley was thirty-six, he could still say, "I
have never published anything yet, but at the desire of
others."   Before he left Oxford, towards the end of 1690,
a friend had already engaged him to appear in print.
The Baroccian collection of manuscripts contained the
only known copy of a chronicle written in Greek by a
certain John of Antioch.   He is sometimes called John
Malelas, or simply Malelas.   This is the Greek form of
a Syriac surname similar in import to the Greek *rhetor*—
"orator," "eloquent writer."   It was given to other literary men also, and merely served to distinguish this John
of Antioch from other well-known men of the same name
and place.   His date is uncertain, but may probably be
placed between the seventh and tenth centuries.   His
chronicle is a work of the kind which was often undertaken by Christian compilers.   Beginning from the Crea-
tion, he sought to give a chronological sketch of universal

history down to his own time. The work, as extant, is incomplete. It begins with a statement characteristic of its general contents: "After the death of Hephaestus (Vulcan), his son Helius (the Sun) reigned over the Egyptians for the space of 4407 days;" and it breaks off at the year 560 A.D., five years before the death of Justinian. Historically it is worthless, except in so far as it preserves a few notices by writers contemporary with the later emperors; and it has no merit of form. Scaliger once described a similar chronicle as a dust-bin. Yet the mass of rubbish accumulated by John of Antioch includes a few fragments of better things. Not only the classical prose-writers but the classical poets were among his authorities, for he made no attempt to discriminate facts from myths. In several places he preserves the names of lost works. Here and there, too, a bit of classical prose or verse has stuck in the dismal swamp of his text. Eager to reconstruct ancient chronology, the students of the seventeenth century had not overlooked this unattractive author. In the reign of Charles I. two Oxford scholars had successively studied him. John Gregory (who died in 1646) had proved the authorship of the chronicle—mutilated though it was at both ends—by showing that a passage of it is elsewhere quoted as from the chronicle of Malelas. Edmund Chilmead—a man remarkable for his attainments in scholarship, mathematics, and music—translated it into Latin, adding notes. As a Royalist, Chilmead was ejected from Christ Church by the Parliamentary Visitation of 1648. He died in 1653, just as his work was ready to be printed. After the lapse of thirty-eight years, the Curators of the Sheldonian Press resolved in 1690 to edit it. The manuscript chronicle had already gained some repute through the citations of it by such scholars as Selden, Usher, Pearson, Stanley, Lloyd. It was arranged that an introduction should be written by Humphrey Hody, who had been James Stillingfleet's College tutor at Wadham, and had, like Bentley, been appointed Chaplain to the Bishop of Worcester. He was an excellent scholar, and performed his task in a highly creditable manner. A general supervision of the edition had been entrusted to Dr. John Mill, Principal of St. Edmund Hall, whose learning has an abiding monument in his subsequent edition of the New Testament. One day Mill and Bentley were walking together at Oxford, when the conversation turned on the chronicle of Malelas. Bentley said that he would like to see the book before it was published. Mill consented, on condition that Bentley would communicate any suggestions that might occur to him. The proof-sheets were then sent to Bentley; who shortly afterwards left Oxford, to take up his residence as chaplain with the Bishop of Worcester.

Dr. Mill presently claimed Bentley's promise; and, thus urged, Bentley at length sent his remarks on Malelas, in the form of a Latin Letter addressed to Dr. Mill. He elsewhere says that he had been further pressed to write it by the learned Bishop Lloyd. In June, 1691, the chronicle appeared, with Bentley's Letter to Mill as an appendix. This edition ("Oxonii, e Theatro Sheldoniano") is a moderately thick octavo volume; first stands a note by Hody, on the spelling of the chronicler's surname; then his Prolegomena, filling 64 pages; the Greek text follows, with Chilmead's Latin version in parallel columns, and foot-notes; and the last 98 pages are occupied by Bentley's Letter to Mill.

Briefly observing that he leaves to Hody the question of the chronicler's identity and age, Bentley comes at

once to the text. Malelas had treated Greek mythology
as history, interweaving it with other threads of ancient
record. Thus, after enumerating some fabulous kings of
Attica, he proceeds: "Shortly afterwards, Gideon was
leader of Israel. Contemporary with him was the famous
lyric poet Orpheus, of Thrace." Malelas then quotes
some statements as to the mystic theology taught by
Orpheus. One of these is a sentence which, as he gives
it, seems to be composed of common words, but is wholly
unintelligible. Bentley takes up this sentence. He shows
that the deeply corrupted words conceal the names of
three mystic divinities in the later Orphic system, sym-
bolical, respectively, of *Counsel*, *Light*, and *Life*. He
proves this emendation, as certain as it is wonderful, by
quoting a passage from Damascius—the last great Neo-
platonist, who lived in the early part of the sixth century,
and wrote a treatise called "Questions and Answers on
First Principles," in which he sketches the theology of
"the current Orphic rhapsodies." This treatise was not
even partially printed till 1828; and Bentley quotes it
from a manuscript in the library of Corpus Christi College, Oxford. He next deals with a group of fictitious
"oracles" which Malelas had reduced from hexameter
verse into prose of the common dialect, and shows that
several of them closely resemble some which he had found
in a manuscript at Oxford, entitled "Oracles and Theolo-
gies of Greek Philosophers."

Then he turns to those passages in which the chronicle
cites the Attic dramatists. He demonstrates the spuriousness of a fragment ascribed to Sophocles. He confirms or
corrects the titles of several lost plays which Malelas ascribes
to Euripides, and incidentally amends numerous passages
which he has occasion to quote. Discursive exuberance of

learning characterises the whole Letter. A single example will serve to illustrate it. Malelas says: "Euripides
brought out a play about Pasiphaë." Bentley remarks
on this: "I do not speak at random; and I am certain
that *no* ancient writer mentions a Pasiphaë of Euripides."
The comic poet Alcæus, indeed, composed a piece of that
name, which is said to have been exhibited in the same
year as the recast *Plutus* of Aristophanes. It is true,
however, Bentley adds, that the *story* of Pasiphaë had
been handled by Euripides, in a lost play called *The Cretans*. This he proves from a scholiast on the *Frogs* of
Aristophanes. But the scholiast himself needs correction:
who says that Euripides introduced Aeropè in *The Cretans*.
Here he is confounding *The Cretans* with another lost
play of Euripides, called the *Women of Crete*: the former
dealt with the story of Icarus and Pasiphaë, the latter
with that of Aeropè, Atreus, and Thyestes. Porphyry,
in his book on Abstinence, quotes nine verses from a play
of Euripides, in which the chorus are addressing Minos.
Grotius, in his Excerpts from Greek Comedies and Tragedies, had attempted to amend these corrupted verses, and
had supposed them to come from the *Women of Crete*.
Bentley (incidentally correcting a grammarian) demonstrates that they can have belonged only to *The Cretans*.
He then turns to the Greek verses themselves. Grotius
had given a Latin version of them, in the same metre.
This metre was the anapæstic—one which had been frequently used by the scholars of the sixteenth and seventeenth centuries, both in translations and in original poems.
Bentley points out that one of its most essential laws had
been ignored, not only by Grotius, but by the modern Latinists generally, including Joseph Scaliger. The ancients
regarded the verses of this metre as forming a continuous

2

chain; hence the last syllable of a verse was not indiffer-
ently long or short, but necessarily one or the other, as if
it occurred in the middle of a verse. Thus Grotius had
written:

> "Quas prisca domos dedit indigena
> Quercus Chalyba secta bipenni."

Here the short *a* at the end of *indigena* should be a
long syllable, in order to make an anapæst (˘˘–). This
is known as Bentley's discovery of the *synaphea* ("*connection*") in anapæstic verse. He further illustrates the
metre from fragments of the Latin poet Attius—which he
amends; one fragment, indeed, he recognises in the prose
of Cicero's *Tusculans*. Returning to the fragment of *The
Cretans* in Porphyry, which Grotius had handled amiss,
Bentley corrects it—with certainty in some points, with
rashness in others, but everywhere brilliantly. Nor has he
done with the verses yet. They mention the *cypress* as
"native" to Crete. This leads Bentley to discuss and
amend passages in Pliny's Natural History, in the History
of Plants by Theophrastus, and in the geographical work
of Solinus.

Elsewhere Malelas refers to the lost *Meleager* of Euripides. Having quoted another mention of it from Hesychius, Bentley takes occasion to show at length the principal
causes of error in that lexicon. This is one of the most
striking parts of the Letter. Then, in numerous places, he
restores proper names which Malelas had defaced. The
chronicler says that the earliest dramatists were Themis,
Minos, and Auleas. Bentley shows that he means Thespis,
Ion of Chios, and Æschylus. Thespis leads him to quote
Clement of Alexandria, and to explain some mysterious
words by showing that they are specimens of a pastime
which consisted in framing a sentence with the twenty-

four letters of the alphabet, each used once only. Speaking of Ion, he gives an exhaustive discussion of that poet's date and writings, verse and prose. The Letter ends with some remarks on the form of the name *Malelas*. Hody had found fault with Bentley for adding the final *s*, which no previous scholar used. *Bentley replies that *a* at the end of a foreign name ordinarily became *as* in Greek—as *Agrippas*. And Malelas being the Greek form of a Greek writer's name, we should keep it in Latin and English, just as Cicero says *Lysias*, not *Lysia*. The Latin exceptions are the domesticated names—those of slaves, or of Greeks naturalised by residence: as *Sosia, Phania*. But it was objected that *Malela* was a "barbarian" name, and therefore indeclinable. Bentley answers that the Hun Attila appears in Greek writers as *Attilas*—adding half a dozen Huns, Goths, and Vandals. The prejudice in favour of *Malela* arose from a simple cause. The chronicler is mentioned only thrice by Greek writers: two of these three passages happen to have the name in the genitive case, which is *Malela;* the third, however, has the nominative, which is *Malelas*. Mr. Hody was not convinced about the *s*. The note—in four large pages of small print—which precedes his Prolegomena was written after he had read Bentley's argument; and ends with a prayer. Mr. Hody's aspiration is that *he* may always write in a becoming spirit; and, finally, that he may be a despiser of trifles (*nugarum denique contemptor*).

Taken as a whole, Bentley's Letter to Mill is an extraordinary performance for a scholar of twenty-eight in the year 1690. It ranges from one topic to another over almost the whole field of ancient literature. Upwards of sixty Greek and Latin writers, from the earliest to the

latest, are incidentally explained or corrected. There are
many curious tokens of the industry with which Bentley
had used his months at Oxford. Thus, referring to a
manuscript of uncertain origin in the Bodleian Library,
"I have made out," he says, "from some iambics at the
beginning—almost effaced by age—that it contains the
work of the grammarian Theognotus, whom the author
of the *Etymologicum Magnum* quotes several times;" and
he gives his proof.

It is interesting to see how strongly this first production
bears the stamp of that peculiar style which afterwards
marked Bentley's criticism. It is less the style of a writer
than of a speaker who is arguing in a strain of rough vivacity with another person. The tone is often as if the
ancient author was reading his composition aloud to Bentley, but making stupid mistakes through drowsiness or in-
attention. Bentley pulls him up short; remonstrates with
him in a vein of good-humoured sarcasm; points out to him
that he can scarcely mean *this*, but—as his own words elsewhere prove—must, no doubt, have meant *that;* and rec-
ommends him to think more of logic. Sometimes it is the
modern reader whom Bentley addresses, as if begging him
to be calm in the face of some tremendous blunder just
committed by the ancient author, who is intended to over-
hear the "aside"—"Do not mind him; he does not really
mean it. He is like this sometimes, and makes us anxious; but he has plenty of good-sense, if one can only get
at it. Let us see what we can do for him." This colloquial manner, with its alternating appeals to author and
reader, in one instance exposed Bentley to an unmerited
rebuke from Dr. Monk. Once, after triumphantly showing that John of Antioch supposed the Bœotian Aulis to

be in Scythia, Bentley exclaims, "*Good indeed, Johnny!*"
(Euge vero, ὦ Ἰωαννίδιον). Dr. Monk thought that this
was said to Dr. John Mill, and reproved it as "an indeco-
rum which neither the familiarity of friendship nor the
license of a dead language can justify towards the digni-
fied Head of a House." Mr. Maehly, in a memoir of Bentley, rejoins: "That may be the view of English high life;
a German savant would never have been offended by the
expressions in question." (Das mag Anschauung des eng-
lischen *high life* sein: einem deutschen Gelehrten würden
die fraglichen Ausdrücke nie aufgefallen sein.) But our
Aristarchus was not addressing the Principal of St. Edmund Hall; he was sportively upbraiding the ancient
chronicler. Indeed, Monk's slip—a thing most rare in his
work—was pointed out in a review of his first edition,
and is absent from the second.

Two of the first scholars of that day—John George
Graevius and Ezechiel Spanheim—separately saluted the
young author of the Letter to Mill as "a new and already
bright star" of English letters. But the Letter to Mill
received by far its most memorable tribute, years after
Bentley's death, from David Ruhnken, in his preface to
the Hesychius of Alberti. "Those great men," he says—
meaning such scholars as Scaliger, Casaubon, Saumaise—
"did not dare to say openly what they thought (about
Hesychius), whether deterred by the established repute
of the grammarian, or by the clamours of the half-learned,
who are always noisy against their betters, and who were
uneasy at the notion of the great Hesychius losing his
pre-eminence. In order that the truth should be published and proved, we needed the learned daring of Richard
Bentley—daring which here, if anywhere, served literature

better than the sluggish and credulous superstition of
those who wish to be called and deemed critics.   Bentley
shook off the servile yoke, and put forth that famous *Letter to Mill*—a wonderful monument of genius and learning, such as could have come only from the first critic of
his time."

CHAPTER II.

ROBERT BOYLE, born in the year after Bacon's death (1627), stands next to him among the Englishmen of the seventeenth century who advanced inductive science. His experiments—"physico-mechanical," as he describes them —led to the discovery of the law for the elasticity of the air; improvements in the air-pump and the thermometer were due to him; and his investigations were serviceable to Hydrostatics, Chemistry, and Medicine. In his theological writings it was his chief aim to show "the reconcilableness of reason and religion," and thus to combat the most powerful prejudice which opposed the early progress of the New Philosophy. Boyle's mind, like Newton's, became more profoundly reverent the further he penetrated into the secrets of nature; his innermost feeling appears to be well represented by the title which he chose for one of his essays—"On the high veneration man's intellect owes to God, peculiarly for his wisdom and power." Thus his "Disquisition of Final Causes" was designed to prove, as against inferences which had been drawn from the cosmical system of Descartes, that the structure of the universe reveals the work of a divine intelligence. Dying on December 30, 1691, he left a bequest which was in har-

mony with the main purpose of his life, and which might
be regarded as his personal and permanent protest against
the idea that a servant of science is an enemy of religion.

He assigned fifty pounds a year as a stipend "for some
divine, or preaching minister," who should "preach eight
Sermons in the year for proving the Christian religion
against notorious infidels, viz. Atheists, Deists, Pagans,
Jews, and Mahometans; *not descending to any controversies
that are among Christians themselves:* The lectures to be
on the first Monday of the respective months of January,
February, March, April, May, September, October, November; in such church as the trustees shall from time to time
appoint." The four trustees named in the will—Bishop
Tenison, Sir Henry Ashurst, Sir John Rotheram, and John
Evelyn (the author of the *Sylva* and the *Diary*)—soon
appointed the Lecturer who was to deliver the first course.
"We made choice of one Mr. Bentley," says Evelyn —
"chaplain to the Bishop of Worcester." Bishop Stillingfleet, himself so eminent an apologist, would naturally
be consulted in such an election.

Bentley took for his subject the first of the topics
indicated by the founder—"A confutation of Atheism."
At this time the *Leviathan* of Thomas Hobbes had been
forty years before the world: and Bentley's lectures stand
in a peculiar relation to it. Hobbes resolved all ideas into
sensations; he denied that there was "any common rule
of good and evil, to be taken from the nature of the objects themselves." He did *not*, however, deny the existence of a God. "Curiosity about causes," says Hobbes,
"led men to search out, one after the other, till they came
to the necessary conclusion, that there is some eternal
cause which men called God. But they have no more
idea of his nature than a blind man has of fire, though he

knows that there is something which warms him." So elsewhere he distinguishes between the necessary " acknowledgment of one infinite, omnipotent, and eternal God," and the attempt—which he pronounces delusive— to define the nature of that Being " by spirit incorporeal."

Bentley held with those who regarded Hobbes, not merely as a materialist who destroyed the basis of morality, but as an atheist in the disguise of a deist. Writing to Bernard, Bentley says roundly of Hobbes, "his corporeal God is a meer sham to get his book printed." Hobbes had said—not in the *Leviathan*, but in " An Answer to Bishop Bramhall," who had pressed him on this point—" I maintain God's existence, and that he is a most pure and most simple *corporeal spirit:*" adding, " by corporeal I mean a substance that has magnitude." Elsewhere he adds *"invisible"* before " corporeal." But at this time the suspicion of a tendency was sometimes enough to provoke the charge of atheism: thus Cudworth, in his *"Intellectual System "*—published fourteen years before Bentley's lectures, and, like them, directed mainly against Hobbes—casts the imputation, without a shadow of reason, on Gassendi, Descartes, and Bacon. Bentley declared that atheism was rife in " taverns and coffee-houses, nay Westminster-hall and the very churches." The school of Hobbes, he was firmly persuaded, was answerable for this. " There may be some Spinosists, or immaterial Fatalists, beyond seas," says Bentley ; " but not one English infidel in a hundred is any other than a Hobbist; which I know to be rank atheism in the private study and select conversation of those men, whatever it may appear abroad." Bentley's Lectures are, throughout, essentially an argument against Hobbes. The set of the lecturer's thoughts may be seen from an illustration used

2*

in his second discourse, where he is arguing against a fortuitous origin of the universe. "If a man should affirm that an ape, casually meeting with pen, ink, and paper, and falling to scribble, did happen to write exactly the *Leviathan* of Thomas Hobbes, would an atheist believe such a story?"

It was from the pulpit of St. Martin's Church, in London, that Bentley delivered his Boyle Lectures. The first was given on March 7, 1692. Bentley announces that his refutation of atheists will not be drawn from those sacred books which, in their eyes, possess no special authority; "but, however, there are other books extant, which they must needs allow of as proper evidence; even the mighty volumes of visible nature, and the everlasting tables of right reason; wherein, if they do not wilfully shut their eyes, they may read their own folly written by the finger of God, in a much plainer and more terrible sentence than Belshazzar's was by the hand upon the wall."

In choosing this ground Bentley was following a recent example. Richard Cumberland, afterwards Bishop of Peterborough, had published in 1672 his "Philosophical Disquisition on the Laws of Nature"—arguing, against the school of Hobbes, that certain immutable principles of moral choice are inherent in the nature of things and in the mind of man. He purposely refrains, however, from appealing to Scripture: the testimony which Cumberland invokes is that of recent science, mathematical or physiological—of Descartes and Huygens, of Willis or Harvey. It is characteristic of Bentley that he chose to draw his weapons from the same armoury. He was already a disciple of strictly theological learning. But in this field, as in others, he declined to use authority as a refuge from logical encounter.

Bentley's first Lecture argues that to adopt atheism is "to choose death and evil before life and good;" that such folly is needless, since religion imposes nothing repugnant to man's faculties or incredible to his reason; that it is also hurtful, both to the individual, whom it robs of the best hope, and to communities, since religion is the basis of society. The second Lecture proceeds to deduce the existence of the Deity from the faculties of the human soul. Hobbes had said: "There is no conception in a man's mind which hath not at first, totally or by parts, been begotten upon the organs of sense: the rest are derived from that original." Bentley, on the contrary, undertakes to prove that "the powers of cogitation, and volition, and sensation, are neither inherent in matter as such, nor producible in matter;" but proceed from "some cogitative substance, some incorporeal inhabitant within us, which we call spirit and soul." As the result of the inquiry, he concludes that there is "an immaterial and intelligent Being, that created our souls; which Being was either eternal itself, or created immediately or ultimately by some other Eternal, that has all those perfections. There is, therefore, originally an eternal, immaterial, intelligent Creator; all which together are the attributes of God alone." Evelyn, who was present at this Lecture, writes of it in his *Diary* (April 4, 1692)—"one of the most learned and convincing discourses I had ever heard." From this point we may date the friendship which till his death in 1706 he steadily entertained for Bentley. The third, fourth and fifth Lectures urge the same inference from the origin and structure of human bodies. Bentley seeks to prove that "the human race was neither from everlasting without beginning; nor owes its beginning to the influence of heavenly bodies; nor to what they call nature, that is, the necessary and mechanical motions of dead senseless matter." His style of argument on the evidence of design in the human structure may be seen from this passage on the organism of the heart:

" If we consider the heart, which is supposed to be the first principle of motion and life, and divide it by our imagination into its constituent parts, its arteries, and veins, and nerves, and tendons, and membranes, and innumerable little fibres that these secondary parts do consist of, we shall find nothing here singular, but what is in any other muscle of the body. 'Tis only the site and posture of these several parts, and the configuration of the whole, that give it the form and functions of a heart. Now, why should the first single fibres in the formation of the heart be peculiarly drawn in spiral lines, when the fibres of all other muscles are made by a transverse rectilinear motion? What could determine the fluid matter into that odd and singular figure, when as yet no other member is supposed to be formed, that might direct the course of that fluid matter? Let mechanism here make an experiment of its power, and produce a spiral and turbinated motion of the whole moved body without an external director."

The last three Lectures (vi., vii., viii.) deal with the proofs from " the origin and frame of the world." These are by far the most striking of the series. Newton's *Principia* had now been published for five years. But, beyond the inner circle of scientific students, the Cartesian system was still generally received. Descartes taught that each planet was carried round the sun in a separate vortex; and that the satellites are likewise carried round by smaller vortices, contained within those of the several planets. Centrifugal motion would constantly impel the planets to fly off in a straight line from the sun; but they are kept in their orbits by the pressure of an outer sphere, consisting of denser particles which are beyond the action of the vortices.

Newton had demolished this theory. He had shown that the planets are held in their orbits by the force of *gravity*, which is always drawing them towards the sun, combined with a *transverse impulse*, which is always projecting them at tangents to their orbits. Bentley takes up Newton's great discovery, and applies it to prove the existence of an Intelligent Providence. Let us grant, he says, that the force of gravity is inherent to matter. What can have been the origin of that other force—the transverse impulse? This impulse is not uniform, but has been adjusted to the place of each body in the system. Each planet has its particular velocity, proportioned to its distance from the sun and to the quantity of the solar matter. It can be due to one cause alone—an intelligent and omnipotent Creator.

This view has the express sanction of Newton. His letters to Bentley — subsequent in date to the Lectures —repeatedly confirm it. "I do not know any power in nature," Newton writes, "which would cause this transverse motion without the divine arm." . . . "To make this system, with all its motions, required a cause which understood and compared together the quantities of matter in the several bodies of the sun and planets, and the gravitating powers resulting from thence; the several distances of the primary planets from the sun, and of the secondary ones from Saturn, Jupiter, and the Earth; and the velocities with which these planets could revolve about those quantities of matter in the central bodies; and to com-

. pare and adjust all these things together, in so great a variety of bodies, argues that cause to be, not blind and fortuitous, but very well skilled in mechanics and geometry."

The application of Newton's discoveries which Bentley makes in the Boyle Lectures was peculiarly welcome to Newton himself. "When I wrote my treatise about our system," he says to Bentley, "I had an eye upon such principles as might work with considering men for the belief of a Deity; and nothing can rejoice me more than to find it useful for that purpose. But if I have done the public any service this way, it is due to nothing but industry and patient thought."

The correspondence between Bentley and Newton, to which the Boyle Lectures gave rise, would alone make them memorable. It has commonly been supposed that Bentley first studied the *Principia* with a view to these Lectures. This, as I can prove, is an error. The Library of Trinity College, Cambridge, contains the autographs of Newton's four letters to Bentley, and of his directions for reading the *Principia;* also a letter to Wotton from John Craig, a Scottish mathematician, giving advice on the same subject, for Bentley's benefit. Now, Craig's letter is dated June 24, 1691; Bentley, then, must have turned his mind to the *Principia* six months before the Boyle Lectures were even founded. We know, further, that in 1689 he was working on Lucretius. I should conjecture, then, that his first object in studying Newton's cosmical system had been to compare it with that of Epicurus, as interpreted by Lucretius; to whom, indeed, he refers more than once in the Boyle Lectures. Craig gives an alarming list of books which must be read before the *Principia* can be understood, and represents the study as most arduous. Newton's own directions to Bentley are simple and en-

couraging: "at ye first perusal of my Book," he concludes, "it's enough if you understand ye Propositions
wth some of ye Demonstrations wch are easier than the
rest. For when you understand ye easier, they will afterwards give you light into ye harder." At the bottom of
the paper Bentley has written, in his largest and bold-
est character, "*Directions from Mr. Newton by his own
Hand.*" There is no date. Clearly, however, it was
Craig's formidable letter which determined Bentley on
writing to Newton. The rapidity with which Bentley—
amongst all his other pursuits—comprehended the *Principia* proves both industry and power. Some years later,
his Lectures were searched for flaws by John Keill, afterwards Savilian Professor of Astronomy at Oxford, and
the principal agent in introducing Newton's system there.
The Phalaris controversy was going on, and Keill wished
to damage Bentley. But he could find only one real blot.
Bentley had missed Newton's discovery—mentioned, but
not prominent, in the *Principia*—that the moon revolves
about her own axis. Keill's only other point was a verbal
cavil, refuted by the context. Better testimony to Bentley's accuracy could scarcely have been borne.

The last Lecture was given on December 5, 1692. The
first six had already been printed. But before publishing
the last two—which dealt in more detail with Newton's
principles—Bentley wished to consult Newton himself.
He therefore wrote to him, at Trinity College, Cambridge.
It was in the autumn of that year that Newton had finished his Letters on Fluxions. He was somewhat out of
health, suffering from sleeplessness and loss of appetite;
perhaps (as his letters to Locke suggest) vexed by the repeated failure of his friends to obtain for him such a provision as he desired. But he at once answered Bentley's

letter with that concise and lucid thoroughness which
makes his style a model in its kind. His first letter is
dated Dec. 10, 1692, and addressed to Bentley "at the
Bishop of Worcester's House, in Park Street in Westminster." On the back of it Bentley has written : " Mr
Newton's Answer to some Queries sent by me, after I had
preach't my 2 last Sermons ; All his answers are agreeable to what I had deliver'd before in the pulpit. But of
some incidental things I do ἐπέχειν [suspend judgment].
R. B." Three other letters are extant which Newton wrote
at this time to Bentley—the last on Feb. 25, 1693. He
probably wrote others also ; there are several from Bentley to him in the Portsmouth collection.

In the course of these four letters, Newton approves
nearly all the arguments for the existence of God which
Bentley had deduced from the *Principia*. On one important point, however, he corrects him. Bentley had
conceded to the atheists that gravity may be essential and
inherent to matter. " Pray," says Newton, "do not as-
cribe that notion to me ; for the cause of gravity is what
I do not pretend to know, and therefore would take more
time to consider of it." In the last letter, about five
weeks later, Newton returns to this topic, and speaks
more decidedly. The notion of gravity being inherent to
matter "is to me," he says, "so great an absurdity, that
I believe no man, who has in philosophical matters any
competent faculty of thinking, can ever fall into it.
Gravity must be caused by an agent acting constantly
according to certain laws ; but whether this agent be material or immaterial, I have left to the consideration of
my readers."

One of the most interesting points in these letters is to
see how a mind like Bentley's, so wonderfully acute in

certain directions, and logical in criticism even to excess, is corrected by a mathematical mind. Thus Bentley, in writing to Newton, had argued that every particle of matter in an infinite space has an infinite quantity of matter on all sides, and consequently an infinite attraction every way; it must therefore rest in equilibrium, all infinites being equal. Now, says Newton, by similar reasoning we might prove that an inch is equal to a foot. For, if an inch may be divided into an infinite number of parts, the sum of those parts will be an inch; and if a foot may be divided into an infinite number of parts, the sum of those parts must be a foot; and therefore, since all infinites are equal, those sums must be equal; that is, an inch must be equal to a foot. The logic is strict; what, then, is the error in the premises? The position, Newton answers, that all infinites are equal. Infinites may be considered in two ways. Viewed absolutely, they are neither equal nor unequal. But when considered under certain definite restrictions, as mathematics may consider them, they can be compared. "A mathematician would tell you that, though there be an infinite number of infinite little parts in an inch, yet there is twelve times that number of such parts in a foot." And so Bentley's infinite attracting forces must be so conceived as if the addition of the slightest finite attracting force to either would destroy the equilibrium.

Johnson has observed that these letters show " how even the mind of Newton gains ground gradually upon darkness :" a fine remark, but one which will convey an incorrect impression if it is supposed to mean that Bentley's questions had led Newton to modify or extend any doctrine set forth in the *Principia*. Bentley's present object in using the *Principia* was to refute atheism.

Newton had not previously considered all the possible applications of his own discoveries to the purposes of theological controversy. This is the limit to the novelty of suggestion which he found in Bentley's letters. Besides the few cases in which Newton points out a fallacy, there are others in which he puts a keener edge on some argument propounded by his correspondent. For instance, Bentley had submitted some reasons against " the hypothesis of deriving the frame of the world by mechanical principles from matter evenly spread through the heavens." This was one of the theories which sought to eliminate the necessity of an intelligent cause. It was, of course, radically incompatible with Newton's system. " I had considered it very little," Newton writes, "before your letters put me upon it." But then he goes on to point out how it may be turned against its authors. It involves the assumption that gravity is inherent to matter. But, if this is so, then matter could never have been evenly spread through the heavens without the intervention of a supernatural power.

Newton's letters, while they heighten our admiration for the master, also illustrate the great ability of the disciple—his strong grasp of a subject which lay beyond the sphere of his familiar studies, and his vigorous originality in the use of new acquisitions. Bentley's Boyle Lectures have a lasting worth which is independent of their scientific value as an argument. In regard to the latter, it may be observed that they bear the mark of their age in their limited conception of a natural law as distinguished from a personal agency. Thus gravitation is allowed as a natural " law " because its action is constant and uniform. But wherever there is a more and a less, wherever the operation is apparently variable, this is explained by the in-

tervening will of an intelligent person; it is not conceived
that the disturbing or modifying force may be another,
though unknown, "law," in the sense in which that name
is given to a manifestly regular sequence of cause and effect. On their literary side, the best parts of the Lectures
exhibit Bentley as a born controversialist, and the worst
as a born litigant. The latter character appears in an occasional tendency to hair-splitting and quibbling; the former, in his sustained power of terse and animated reasoning, in rapid thrust and alert defence, in ready command
of various resources, in the avoidance of declamation while
he is proving his point, and in the judicious use of eloquence to clinch it. Here, as elsewhere, he has the knack
of illustrating an abstruse subject by an image from common things. He is touching (in the second Lecture) on
the doctrine of Epicurus that our freedom of will is due
to the declension of atoms from the perpendicular as they
fall through infinite space. "'Tis as if one should say
that a bowl equally poised, and thrown upon a plain and
smooth bowling-green, will run necessarily and fatally in a
direct motion; but if it be made with a bias, that may de-
cline it a little from a straight line, it may acquire by that
motion a liberty of will, and so run spontaneously to the
jack." It may be noticed that a passage in the eighth
Lecture is one of the quaintest testimonies in literature to
the comparatively recent origin of a taste for the grander
forms of natural scenery. Bentley supposes his adversaries to object that "the rugged and irregular surface" of
the earth refutes its claim to be "a work of divine artifice."
"We ought not to believe," he replies, "that the banks of
the ocean are really deformed, because they have not the
form of a regular bulwark; nor that the mountains are out
of shape, because they are not exact pyramids or cones."

The Lectures made a deep and wide impression. Soon
after they had been published, a Latin version appeared
at Berlin.   A Dutch version subsequently came out at
Utrecht.   There was one instance, indeed, of dissent from
the general approval.   A Yorkshire squire wrote a pamphlet, intimating that his own experience did not lead him
to consider the faculties of the human soul as a decisive
argument for the existence of a Deity; and, referring to
Bentley's observations on this head, he remarked, " I judge
he hath taken the wrong sow by the ear."   In 1694
Bentley again delivered a course of Boyle Lectures—" A
Defence of Christianity "—but they were never printed.
Manuscript copies of them are mentioned by Kippis, the
editor of the *Biographia Britannica* (1780); but Dean
Vincent, who died in 1815, is reported by Kidd as believ-
ing that they were lost.

CHAPTER III.

LEARNED CORRESPONDENCE.—THE KING'S LIBRARIAN.

IN 1692—the year of his first Boyle Lecturership—an accident placed Bentley in correspondence with John George Graevius, a German who held a professorship at Utrecht, and stood in the front rank of classical—especially Latin —scholarship. When Bentley was seeking materials for an edition of Manilius, he received a box of papers from Sir Edward Sherburn, an old Cavalier who had partly translated the poet. The papers in the box, bought at Antwerp, had belonged to the Dutch scholar, Gaspar Gevärts. Amongst them was a Latin tract by Albert Rubens ("Rubenius,") the author of another treatise which Graevius had previously edited. Bentley, with Sherburn's leave, sent the newly-found tract to Graevius, who published it in 1694, with a dedication to Bentley. This circumstance afterwards brought on Bentley the absurd charge of having intercepted an honour due to Sherburn.

Graevius was rejoiced to open a correspondence with the author of the Letter to Mill, which he had warmly admired. The professor's son had lately died, leaving an unpublished edition of the Greek poet Callimachus, which Graevius was now preparing to edit. He applied to Bentley for any literary aid that he could give. In reply,

Bentley undertook to collect the fragments of Callimachus, scattered up and down throughout Greek literature;
remarking that he could promise to double the number
printed in a recent Paris edition, and also to improve the
text.   In 1696 Bentley fulfilled this promise by sending
to Graevius a collection of about 420 fragments; also a
new recension of the poet's epigrams, with additions to
their number from a fresh manuscript source, and with
some notes on the hymns.   The edition appeared at
Utrecht in 1697, with Bentley's contributions.

In the preface Graevius shows his sense that the work
done by Bentley—"that new and brilliant light of Brit-
ain"—was not merely excellent in quality, but of a new
order.   Such indeed it was.   Since then, successive generations have laboured at collecting and sifting the fragments of the Greek poets.   But in 1697 the world had
no example of systematic work in this field.   The first
pattern of thorough treatment and the first model of critical method were furnished by Bentley's Callimachus.
Hitherto the collector of fragments had aimed at little
more than heaping together "the limbs of the dismem-
bered poet."   Bentley shows how these limbs, when they
have been gathered, may serve, within certain limits, to reconstruct the body.   Starting from a list of the poet's
works, extant or known by title, he aims at arranging the
fragments under those works to which they severally belonged.   But, while he concentrates his critical resources
in a methodical manner, he wisely refrains from pushing
conjecture too far.   His Callimachus is hardly more distinguished by brilliancy than by cautious judgment—praise
which could not be given to all his later works.   Here, as
in the Letter to Mill, we see his metrical studies bearing
fruit: thus he points out a fact which had hitherto es-

caped even such scholars as Saumaise and Casaubon—
that the Greek diphthongs *ai* and *oi* cannot be shortened
before consonants. Ernesti, in the preface to his Callimachus (1763), speaks of Bentley as "having distanced competition :" and another estimate, of yet higher authority,
is expressed more strongly still. "Nothing more excellent in its kind has appeared," said Valckenaer—"nothing
more highly finished ;" "a most thorough piece of work,
by which writers who respect their readers might well be
deterred" from an attempt at rivalry. It is no real abate-
ment of Bentley's desert that a few gleanings were left for
those who came after him. Here, as in some other cases,
the distinctive merit of his work is not that it was final,
but that it was exemplary. In this particular department
—the editing of fragments—he differed from his predecessors as the numismatist, who arranges a cabinet of coins,
differs from the digger who is only aware that he has un-
earthed an old bit of gold or silver.

Meanwhile letters had been passing between Bentley and
a correspondent very unlike Graevius. In 1693 Joshua
Barnes, of Emmanuel College, Cambridge, was editing Euripides, and wrote to Bentley, asking his reasons for an
opinion attributed to him—that the "Letters of Euripides" were spurious. Bentley gave these reasons in a long
and courteous reply. Barnes, however, resented the loss
of a cherished illusion. Not only did he omit to thank
Bentley, but in the preface to his Euripides (1694) he alluded to his correspondent's opinion as "a proof of ef-
frontery or incapacity." Barnes is a curious figure, half
comic, half pathetic, amongst the minor persons of Bentley's story. Widely read, incessantly laborious, but un-
critical and vain, he poured forth a continual stream of
injudicious publications, English or Greek, until, when he

was fifty-one, they numbered forty-three. The last work of his life was an elaborate edition of Homer. He had invested the fortune of Mrs. Barnes in this costly enterprise, obtaining her somewhat reluctant consent, it was said, by representing the "Iliad" as the work of King Solomon. Queen Anne declined the dedication, and nothing could persuade poor Barnes that this was not Bentley's doing. Bentley said of Barnes that he probably knew about as much Greek, and understood it about as well, as an Athenian blacksmith. The great critic appears to have forgotten that Sophocles and Aristophanes were appreciated by audiences which represented the pit and the gallery much more largely than the boxes and the stalls. An Athenian blacksmith could teach us a good many things.

Bentley had now made his mark, and he had powerful friends. One piece of preferment after another came to him. In 1692 Bishop Stillingfleet procured for him a prebendal stall at Worcester, and three years later appointed him to hold the Rectory of Hartlebury, in that county, until James Stillingfleet should be in full orders. At the end of the year 1693 the office of Royal Librarian became vacant. By an arrangement which was not then thought singular, the new Librarian was induced to resign in favour of Bentley, who was to pay him £130 a year out of the salary of £200. The patent appointing Bentley Keeper of the Royal Libraries bore date April 12, 1694. The "Licensing Act" (Stat. 13 and 14, Car. II.) finally expired in 1694, a few months after Bentley took office. But he made the most of his time. The Act reserved three copies of every book printed in England—one for the Royal Library, one for Oxford, and one for Cambridge. Latterly it had been evaded. Bentley applied to the Master of the Stationers' Company, and exacted "*near a thousand*" volumes. In this year he was elected a Fellow of the Royal Society. In 1695 he became a Chaplain in ordinary to the King. Hitherto he had resided with Bishop Stillingfleet; but early in 1696 he took possession of the rooms in St. James's Palace which were assigned to the Royal Librarian.

One of his letters to Evelyn—whom he had been helping to revise his *Numismata*, a "Discourse on Medals, ancient and modern"—discloses an amusing incident. Bentley's lodgings at St. James's were next the Earl of Marlborough's. Bentley wished to annex some rooms overhead, for the better bestowal of certain rare books. Marlborough undertook to plead his cause. The result of this obliging diplomacy was that the future hero of Blenheim got "the closets" for himself. Bentley now became anxious to build a new library, and Evelyn warmly sympathises with his "glorious enterprise." It was, indeed, much needed. The books were so ill-lodged that they could not be properly arranged; Bentley declared that the library was "not fit to be seen;" and he kept its chief treasure, the Alexandrine MS. of the Greek Bible, at his own rooms in the palace, "for this very reason, that persons might see it without seeing the library." The Treasury consented to the proposal for building. But public business prevented the bill coming before Parliament, and the scheme was dropped for the time. Meanwhile Bentley's energy found scope at Cambridge. Since the civil troubles, the University Press had lapsed into a state which called for reparation. Bentley took an active part in procuring subscriptions for that purpose. He was empowered by the University to order new founts of type, which were cast in Holland. Evelyn, in his *Diary* (Aug. 17, 1696), alludes to "that noble presse which my worthy and most learned

3

friend . . . is with greate charge and industrie erecting
now at Cambridge." In the same year Bentley took
the degree of Doctor in Divinity. On Commencement
Sunday (July 5, 1696) he preached before the University,
taking as his text 1 Pet. iii. 15. The sermon, which is extant, defends Christianity against deism.

It is natural to ask—was Bentley yet remarked for any
of those qualities which form the harsher side of his character in later life? He was now thirty-four. There is the
story of the dinner-party at Bishop Stillingfleet's, at which
the guest, who had been sitting next Bentley, said to the
Bishop after dinner, " My Lord, that chaplain of yours is
certainly a very extraordinary man." (Mr. Bentley, like
the chaplain in " Esmond," had doubtless conformed to the
usage of the time, and retired when the custards appeared.)
" Yes," said Stillingfleet, " had he but the gift of humility,
he would be the most extraordinary man in Europe." If
this has a certain flavour of concoction, at any rate there
is no doubt as to what Pepys wrote, after reading Boyle's
allusion to Bentley's supposed discourtesy. " I suspect
Mr. Boyle is in the right; for our friend's learning (which
I have a great value for) wants a little filing." Against
such hints there is a noteworthy fact to be set. A letter
of Bentley's to Evelyn, dated Oct. 21, 1697, mentions that
a small group of friends had arranged to meet in the even-
ings, once or twice a week, at Bentley's lodgings in St.
James's. These are the names: John Evelyn, Sir Christopher Wren, John Locke, Isaac Newton. A person with
whom such men chose to place themselves in frequent and
familiar intercourse must have been distinguished by something else than insolent erudition. But now we must see
how Bentley bore himself in the first great crisis of his
career.

CHAPTER IV.

THE CONTROVERSY ON THE LETTERS OF PHALARIS.

WILLIAM WOTTON'S *Reflections on Ancient and Modern Learning* (1694) give the best view of a discussion which greatly exercised the wits of the day. "Soon after the Restauration of King Charles II.," says Wotton, "upon the institution of the Royal Society, the comparative excellency of the Old and New Philosophy was eagerly debated in England. But the disputes then managed between Stubbe and Glanvile were rather particular, relating to the Royal Society, than general, relating to knowledge in its utmost extent. In France this controversy has been taken up more at large. The French were not content to argue the point in Philosophy and Mathematicks, but even in Poetry and Oratory too; where the Ancients had the general opinion of the learned on their side. Monsieur de Fontenelle, the celebrated author of a Book concerning the Plurality of Worlds, began the dispute about six years ago [1688], in a little Discourse annexed to the *Pastorals*."

Perrault, going further still than Fontenelle, "in oratory sets the Bishop of Meaux [Bossuet] against Pericles (or rather Thucydides), the Bishop of Nismes [Fléchier] against Isocrates, F. Bourdaloue against Lysias, Monsieur Voiture against Pliny, and Monsieur Balzac against Cicero. In

Poetry likewise he sets Monsieur Boileau against Horace,
Monsieur Corneille and Monsieur Molière against the Ancient Dramatic Poets."

Sir William Temple, in his "Essay on Ancient and
Modern Learning"—published in 1692, and dedicated to
his own University, *Almæ Matri Cantabrigiensi*—was not
less uncompromising in the opposite direction. His general view is that the Ancients surpassed the Moderns, not
merely in art and literature, but also in every branch of
science, though the records of their science have perished.
"The Moderns," Temple adds, "gather all their learning
out of Books in the Universities." The Ancients, on the
contrary, travelled with a view to original research, and
advanced the limits of knowledge in their subjects by per-
sistent interviews with reserved specialists in foreign parts.
Thales and Pythagoras are Sir William's models in this
way. "Thales acquired his knowledge in Egypt, Phœ-
nicia, Delphos, and Crete; Pythagoras spent twenty-two
years in Egypt, and twelve years more in Chaldæa; and
then returned laden with all their stores." Temple's performance was translated into French, and made quite a
sensation in the Academy—receiving, amongst other trib-
utes, the disinterested homage of the Modern Horace.

Wotton's object was to act as a mediator, and "give to
every side its just due." As to "eloquence and poetry,"
it required some courage (in England) even to hint that
the Moderns had beaten the Ancients. "It is almost a
heresie in wit, among our poets, to set up any modern
name against Homer or Virgil, Horace or Terence. So
that though here and there one should in Discourse prefer
the writers of the present age, yet scarce any man among
us, who sets a value upon his own reputation, will venture
to assert it in print." With regard to science, however,

Wotton speaks out, and in a gentle way disposes of the
Ancients. He may, in fact, claim the credit of having
made a sensible contribution to the discussion. Sir William Temple, "the ornament of the age," was no mean
antagonist. Wotton must have been glad of a trusty ally,
especially on the ground of ancient literature, the strongest
part of the enemy's position. Such an ally he found in
Bentley. Temple had written thus:

"It may perhaps be further affirmed, in favour of the
Ancients, that the oldest books we have are still in their
kind the best. The two most ancient that I know of in
prose, among those we call profane authors, are Æsop's
Fables and Phalaris's Epistles, both living near the same
time, which was that of Cyrus and Pythagoras. As the
first has been agreed by all ages since for the greatest master in his kind, and all others of that sort have been but
imitations of his original; so I think the Epistles of Phalaris to have more race, more spirit, more force of wit and
genius, than any others I have ever seen, either ancient or
modern. I know several learned men (or that usually pass
for such, under the name of critics) have not esteemed
them genuine; and Politian, with some others, have attributed them to Lucian: but I think he must have little
skill in painting that cannot find out this to be an original.
Such diversity of passions, upon such variety of actions
and passages of life and government; such freedom of
thought, such boldness of expression; such bounty to his
friends, such scorn of his enemies; such honour of learned
men, such esteem of good; such knowledge of life, such
contempt of death; with such fierceness of nature and
cruelty of revenge, could never be represented but by him
that possessed them. And I esteem Lucian to have been
no more capable of writing than of acting what Phalaris

did. In all one writ you find the scholar or the sophist; in all the other, the tyrant and the commander."

Mutual admiration and modern journalism have seldom produced a more magnificent advertisement than Sir William Temple had given to this ancient writer. After the slumber, or the doze, of centuries, Phalaris awoke and found himself in demand. The booksellers began to feel an interest in him such as they had never even simulated before.

The "Epistles of Phalaris" are a collection of a hundred and forty-eight letters—many of them only a few lines long—written in "Attic" Greek of that artificial kind which begins to appear about the time of Augustus. They are first mentioned by a Greek writer, Stobæus, who flourished about 480 A.D. We know nothing about the exact time at which they were written. On the other hand there is no doubt as to the class of literature which they represent, or the general limits of the period to which they must be assigned. These limits are roughly marked by the first five centuries of the Christian era.

Phalaris, the reputed author of the Letters, is a shadowy figure in the early legends of ancient Sicily. The modern Girgenti, on the south-west coast of the island, preserves the name of Agrigentum, as the Romans called the Greek city of Akragas. Founded early in the sixth century before Christ by a Dorian colony from Gela, Akragas stood on the spacious terraces of a lofty hill. It was a splendid natural stronghold. Steep cliffs were the city's bulwarks on the south; on the north, a craggy ridge formed a rampart behind it, and the temple-crowned citadel, a precipitous rock, towered to a height of twelve hundred feet above the sea. Story told that Phalaris, a citizen of Akragas, had contrived to seize the citadel, and to make himself absolute ruler of the place—in Greek phrase, "tyrant." He strengthened the city—then recently founded—and was successful in wars upon his neighbours. At last his own subjects rose against him, overthrew his power, and put him to death. This latter event is said to have occurred between 560 and 550 B.C. Such was the tradition. All that we really know about Phalaris, however, is that as early as about 500 B.C. his name had become a proverb for horrible cruelty, not only in Sicily, but throughout Hellas. Pindar refers to this in his first Pythian ode (474 B.C.): "the kindly worth of Crœsus fades not; but in every land hate follows the name of *him who burned men in a brazen bull, the ruthless Phalaris.*"

This habit of slowly roasting objectionable persons in a brazen bull was the only definite trait which the Greeks of the classical age associated with Phalaris. And this is the single fact on which Lucian founds his amusing piece, in which envoys from Phalaris offer the bull to the temple of Delphi, and a Delphian casuist urges that it ought to be accepted. The bull may be seen, portrayed by the fancy of a modern artist, in the frontispiece to Charles Boyle's edition of the Letters. The head of the brazen animal is uplifted, as if it was bellowing; one of the tyrant's apparitors is holding up the lid of a large oblong aperture in the bull's left flank; two others are hustling in a wretched man, who has already disappeared, all but his legs. The two servants wear the peculiar expression of countenance which may be seen on the faces of persons engaged in packing; meanwhile another pair of slaves, with more animated features, are arranging the fagots under the bull, which are already beginning to blaze cheerfully, so that a gentle warmth must be felt on the inner surface of the brass, though it will probably be

some minutes yet before it begin to be uncomfortable.
Phalaris is seated on his throne just behind the bull, in a
sort of undress uniform, with a long round ruler for scep-
tre in his right hand; firmness and mildness are so blend-
ed in his aspect that it is impossible not to feel in the
presence of a great and good man; on the left side of the
throne, a Polonius is standing a little in the background,
with a look of lively edification subdued by deference;
and in the distance there is a view of hills and snug farm-
houses, suggesting fair rents and fixity of tenure.

The rather hazy outlines of the old Greek tradition are
filled up by Phalaris himself in the Letters, which abound
with little bits of autobiography. He gives us to know
that he was born—not at Agrigentum, as Lucian has it—
but at a place called Astypalæa, seemingly a town in
Crete. He got into trouble there at an early age, being
suspected of aiming at a tyranny, and was banished, leaving his wife and son behind him; when he betook himself to Agrigentum, and there became a farmer of taxes;
obtained the management of a contract for building a
temple on the rocky height above the town; hired troops
with the funds thus committed to him; and so made himself master of the place. Some of the letters are to his
wife, his son, and a few of his particular friends, among
whom is the poet Stesichorus. One or two epistles are
addressed to distinguished strangers, begging them to
come and see him in Sicily—as to Pythagoras, and Abaris
the Hyperborean; and, what is very curious, the collection gives us the answer sent by Abaris, which refers not
obscurely to the bull, and declines the invitation of the
prince in language more forcible than polite. Then there
are a few letters to various communities—the people of
Messene, the people of Tauromenion, and others.

It may be well to give a short specimen or two. Not a few of the Letters, it should be premised, are pervaded by a strain of allusion to the bull. Phalaris was a person of almost morbid sensibility, and if there was one subject on which he was more alive to innuendo than another it was this of the bull, and the want of regard for the feelings of others which his use of it had been thought to imply. There are moments when he can no longer suffer in silence, but comes to the point, as in the following letter to the Athenians [Ep. 122 = 5 (Lennep)]:

"Your artist Perilaus, Athenians, came to me with some works of very satisfactory execution; on account of which we gladly received him, and requited him with worthy gifts, for the sake of his art, and more particularly for the sake of his native city. Not long since, however, he made a brazen bull of more than natural size, and brought it to Akragas. Now we were delighted to welcome an animal whose labours are associated with those of man; the effigy appeared a most proper gift to a prince—a noble object of art; for he had not yet disclosed to us the death which lurked within. But when he opened a door in the flank, and laid bare

'Murder fulfilled of perfect cruelty,
A fate more dire than all imagined death,'

then, indeed, after praising him for his skill, we proceeded to punish him for his inhumanity. We resolved to make him the first illustration of his own device, since we had never met with a worse villain than its contriver. So we put him into the bull, and lit the fire about it, according to his own directions for the burning. Cruel was his science; stern the proof to which he brought it. We did not see the sufferer; we heard not his cries or lamenta-

3*

tions; for the human shrieks that resounded within came
forth to his listening punishers as the bellowings of a brazen throat.

"Now, Athenians, when I was informed that you resented the removal of your artist, and were incensed with
me, I felt surprise; and for the present I am unable to
credit the report. If you censure me on the ground that
I did not torment him by a more cruel mode of death,
I reply that no mode more cruel has yet occurred to me;
if, on the other hand, you blame me for having punished him at all, then your city, which glories in its humanity, courts the charge of extreme barbarity. The
bull was the work of one Athenian, or of all: but this
will be decided by your disposition towards me.... If
you consider the case dispassionately, you will perceive
that I act involuntarily; and that, if Providence decrees
that I must suffer, my lot will be unmerited. Though
my royal power gives me free scope of action, I still rec-
ognize that measures of a harsh tendency are exceptional;
and, though I cannot revoke the deeds of the past, I can
confess their gravity. Would, however, that I had never
been compelled to them by a hard necessity! In that
case, no one else would have been named for his virtues
where Phalaris was in company."

The following letter, addressed by Phalaris to a peevish
critic, shows that consciousness of rectitude had gradually
braced the too sensitive mind of the prince [Ep. 66=94
(Lennep)]:

"To Telecleides.

"For reasons best known to yourself, you have repeatedly observed in conversation with my friends that, after
the death of Perilaus, the artist of the bull, I ought not
to have despatched any other persons by the same mode

of torment; since I thus cancel my own merit. Possibly you had in view the result which has actually occurred—viz., that your remarks should be carried to me. Now, as to Perilaus, I do not value myself upon the compliments which I received for having punished him; praise was not my object in assuming that office. As to the other persons, I feel no uneasiness at the misrepresentations to which I am exposed for chastising them. Retribution operates in a sphere apart from good or evil report. Permit me, however, to observe that my reason for correcting the artist was precisely this—that other persons *were* to be despatched in the bull. . . . Well, I am now in possession of your views; it is unnecessary for you to trouble other listeners; do but cease to worry yourself and me."

The slight testiness which appears at the end only confirms Sir William Temple's remark, that here we have to do with a man of affairs, whose time was not to be at the mercy of every idle tattler. After Wotton had published the first edition of his "Reflections on Ancient and Modern Learning" (1694), Bentley had happened to speak with him of the passage in Temple's Essay which we quoted above. Bentley observed that the Letters of Phalaris could be proved to be spurious, and that nothing composed by Æsop was extant: opinions which he had formed, and intimated, long before Temple wrote. Wotton then obtained a promise from Bentley that he would give his reasons for these views in a paper to be printed as an appendix to the second edition of the "Reflections." But meanwhile an incident occurred which gave a new turn to the matter.

Dr. Henry Aldrich, then Dean of Christ Church, had been accustomed to engage the most promising of the younger scholars in the task of editing classical authors, and copies of such editions were usually presented by him to members of the House at the beginning of the year. Temple's essay had attracted attention to the Letters of Phalaris. In 1693 the preparation of a new edition was proposed by the Dean to "a young Gentleman of great hopes" (as Bentley calls him), the Honourable Charles Boyle, a brother of the Earl of Orrery, and grand-nephew of Robert Boyle, the founder of the Lectures. Charles Boyle was at this time only seventeen. Before coming to Oxford, he had been the private pupil of Dr. Gale, the Dean of York (formerly, for a brief space, Greek Professor at Cambridge), of whom he says: "the foundation of all the little knowledge I have in these matters was laid by him, which I gratefully own." Boyle's scholarship seems to have been quite up to the higher school standard of that day; he appears to have been bright, clever, and amiable, and was personally much liked at Christ Church. In preparing his Phalaris, he wished to consult a manuscript which was in the King's Library at St. James's. He accordingly wrote to his bookseller in London, Mr. Thomas Bennet, "at the Half-moon in St. Paul's Churchyard," requesting him to get the manuscript collated. This was apparently in September, 1693. Bentley had then nothing to do with the Library. The Royal Patent constituting him Keeper of His Majesty's Libraries bore date April 12, 1694; and, owing to delays of form, it was the beginning of May before he had actual custody of the Library at St. James's. Bennet had already spoken to Bentley (early in 1694, it seems) about the manuscript of Phalaris; and Bentley had replied that he would gladly "help Mr. Boyle to the book."

Meanwhile Bennet had received urgent applications from Boyle, and had laid the blame of the delay on Bentley.

As soon as the latter had assumed charge of the Library (May, 1694), he gave the manuscript to a person sent for it by Bennet. "I ordered him," says Bentley, "to tell the collator not to lose any time; for I was shortly to go out of town for two months." This was afterwards proved by a letter from Gibson, the person employed as collator. The manuscript remained in Gibson's hands "five or six days," according to Bentley; and this estimate can scarcely be excessive, for Boyle himself says merely "not *nine*." Bentley was to leave London for Worcester (to reside two months there) at five o'clock on a Monday morning towards the end of May. On the Saturday before, about noon, Bentley went to Bennet's shop, asked for the manuscript, and waited whilst a message was sent to Gibson. Word came back that Gibson had not finished the collation. Bennet then begged that the manuscript might be left with him till Sunday morning, and promised to make the collator sit up all night. Bentley declined to comply with this demand, but said that they might keep the manuscript till the evening of that day—Saturday. On Saturday evening it was restored to Bentley. Only forty-eight letters had then been collated.

As this affair was made a grave charge against Bentley, it is well to see just what it means. The business of the collator was to take a printed text of Phalaris, compare it with the manuscript, and note those readings in which the manuscript differed from it. This particular manuscript was, in Bentley's words, "as legible as print." "I had a mind," he says, "for the experiment's sake, to collate the first forty epistles, which are all that the collator has done. And I had finished them in an hour and eighteen minutes; though I made no very great haste. And yet I remarked and set down above fifty various lections, though the edi-

tor has taken notice of one only." This manuscript contains only 127 of the 148 letters. At Bentley's rate, the
whole might have been done in about five hours. Suppose that Bentley worked thrice as fast as Gibson; the
latter would have required fifteen hours. Grant, further,
that Gibson had the manuscript for four days only, though
Boyle's phrase, "less than nine," implies eight. He could
still have completed his task by working less than four
hours a day. So utterly groundless was the complaint
that Bentley had not allowed sufficient time for the use
of the manuscript.

That, however, was the defence which Bennet made to
his employer. Clearly he had no liking for the new Librarian who had begun by exacting the dues of the Royal
Library. And he supported it by representing Bentley as
unfriendly to Boyle's work. "The bookseller once asked
me privately," says Bentley, "that I would do him the favour to tell my opinion, if the new edition of Phalaris,
then in the press, would be a vendible book? for he had
a concern in the impression, and hoped it would sell well;
such a great character being given of it in [Temple's] Essays as made it mightily inquired after. I told him, He
would be safe enough, since he was concerned for nothing
but the sale of the book: for the great names of those
that recommended it would get it many buyers. But
however, under the rose, the book was a spurious piece,
and deserved not to be spread in the world by another
impression." Dr. William King, a member of Christ
Church, and a "wit," chanced to be in Bennet's shop one
day, and overheard some remark of Bentley's which he
considered rude towards Boyle. "After he [Bentley] was
gone," writes the frank Dr. King, "I told Mr. Bennet that
he ought to send Mr. Boyle word of it." Boyle's edition

of Phalaris appeared in January, 1695, with a graceful dedication to the Dean of Christ Church. The Latin preface concludes thus:

"I have collated the Letters themselves with two Bodleian manuscripts from the Cantuar and Selden collection; I have also procured a collation, as far as Letter XL., of a manuscript in the Royal Library; the Librarian, with that courtesy which distinguishes him [*pro singulari sua humanitate*], refused me the further use of it. I have not recorded every variation of the MSS. from the printed texts; to do so would have been tedious and useless; but, wherever I have departed from the common reading, my authority will be found in the notes. This little book is indebted to the printer for more than usual elegance; it is hoped that the author's labour may bring it an equal measure of acceptance."

Pro singulari sua humanitate. with that courtesy which distinguishes him; or, as Bentley renders it, with grim literalness, "out of his singular humanity!" This, says Bentley, "was meant as a lash for me, who had the honour then and since to serve his Majesty in that office" (of Librarian); and, in fact, the nature of Bentley's "humanity" forthwith became a question of the day.

The tone of Boyle's public reference to Bentley was wholly unjustifiable. Bentley had returned from Worcester to London some months before Boyle's book was ready, but no application had been made to him for a further use of the manuscript, though a few hours would have finished the collation. Bentley, after his return to London, spent a fortnight at Oxford, "conversing," he says, "in the very college where the editors resided; not the least whisper there of the manuscript." It was on January 26—when the book had been out more than three

weeks—that Bentley chanced to see it for the first time,
" in the hands of a person of honour to whom it had been
presented; and the rest of the impression was not yet
published. This encouraged me to write the very same
evening to Mr. Boyle at Oxford, and to give him a true information of the whole matter; expecting that, upon the
receipt of my letter, he would put a stop to the publication
of his book, till he had altered that passage, and printed
the page anew; which he might have done in one day,
and at the charge of five shillings. I did not expressly
desire him to take out that passage, and reprint the whole
leaf; that I thought was too low a submission. But I
said enough to make any person of common justice and
ingenuity [ingenuousness] have owned me thanks for pre-
venting him from doing a very ill action." " After a delay of two posts," Boyle replied in terms of which Bentley
gives the substance thus: "that what I had said in my
own behalf might be true; but that Mr. Bennet had represented the thing quite otherwise. If he had had my account before, he should have considered of it: and [but?]
now that the book was made public, he would not inter-
pose, but that I might do myself right in what method I
pleased." On receiving Bentley's explanation, Boyle was
clearly bound, if not to withdraw the offensive passage, at
least to stop its circulation until he had inquired further.
And he knew this, as his own words show. This is his
account of his reply to Bentley: " That Mr. Bennet, whom
I employed to wait on him in my name, gave me such an
account of his reception, that I had reason to apprehend
myself affronted: and since I could make no other excuse
to my reader, for not collating the King's MS., but because
'twas denied me, I thought I cou'd do no less than express
some resentment of that denial. That I shou'd be very

much concern'd if Mr. Bennet had dealt so ill with me as to mislead me in his accounts; *and if that appear'd, shou'd be ready to take some opportunity of begging his* [Bentley's] *pardon: and, as I remember, I express'd myself so, that the Dr might understand I meant to give him satisfaction as publickly as I had injur'd him. Here the matter rested, and I thought that Dr Bentley was satisfied.*"

That is to say, Boyle had offered a public affront to Bentley, without inquiring whether Bennet's story was true; Bentley explained that it was untrue; and Boyle still refused to make any amend, even provisionally. Bentley was advised by some of his friends to refute the aspersion: which, indeed, was not merely a charge of rudeness, but also of failure in his duty as Librarian. He remained silent. "Out of a natural aversion to all quarrels and broils, and out of regard to the editor himself, I resolved to take no notice of it, but to let the matter drop."

But in 1697 Wotton was preparing a second edition of the "Reflections," and claimed Bentley's old promise to write something on Æsop and Phalaris. Then, in a great hurry, Bentley wrote an essay on the "Epistles of Phalaris, Themistocles, Socrates, Euripides, and others; and the Fables of Æsop." This essay was printed, with a separate title-page, at the end of the new edition of the "Reflections" (1697). What was he to say about Boyle? "Upon such an occasion," he remarks, "I was plainly obliged to speak of that calumny: for my silence would have been interpreted as good as a confession: especially considering with what industrious malice the story had been spread all over England." In this he was possibly right; it is not easy to say now. But his mode of self-vindication was certainly not judicious. He ought to have confined himself to a statement of the facts concerning the loan of

the manuscript.   After doing this, however, he enters upon
a hostile review of Boyle's book.   Throughout it he speaks
in the plural of " our editors."   He may have had reason
to know that Boyle had been assisted ; but such a use of
the knowledge was unwarrantable.

Boyle's edition was the slight performance of a very
young man, and apart from the sentence in the preface,
might fairly be regarded as privileged.   It contains a short
Latin life of Phalaris, based on ancient notices and on the
Letters themselves ; the Greek text, with a Latin version ;
and, at the end, some notes.   These notes deserve mention
only because Bentley was afterwards accused of having
" pillaged " them.   There was a singular hardihood in this
charge.   Boyle's notes on the hundred and forty-eight Letters occupy just twelve small pages.   The greater part of
them are simply brief paraphrases intended to bring out
the sense of the text.   Three Latin translations of Phalaris
then existed ; one, not printed, but easily accessible in
manuscript, by Francesco Accolti of Arezzo (Aretino) ; a
second, printed by Thomas Kirchmeier, who Hellenized
his surname into Naogeorgus (Basel, 1558) ; and a third,
ascribed to Cujas, which Boyle knew as re-issued at Ingol-
stadt in 1614 for the use of the Jesuit schools.   Boyle's
version occasionally coincides with phrases of Aretino or
the Jesuit text ; this, however, may well be accident.   It
is manifest, however, that his translation was based on that
of Naogeorgus, who is sometimes less elegant, but not
seldom more accurate.

The story of the controversy has usually been told as if
Boyle defended the genuineness of the Letters, while Bentley impugned it.   That is certainly the impression which
any one would derive from Bentley's Dissertation, with its
banter of " our editors and their Sicilian prince."   Proba-

bly it will be new to most persons that Boyle had never asserted the genuineness of the Letters. On the contrary, he had expressly stated some reasons for believing that they were not genuine.

I translate the following from Boyle's Latin preface:

> "The reader of these Letters will find less profit in inquiring who wrote them than pleasure in enjoying the perusal. As to the authorship, the conflicting opinions of learned men must be consulted—perhaps in vain; as to the worth of the book, the reader can judge best for himself. Lest I disappoint curiosity, however—though the controversy does not deserve keen zeal on either part—I will briefly explain what seems to me probable on both sides of the question."

Here he enumerates: (1) some of those who think the Letters genuine—including Sir W. Temple, whose encomium on Phalaris he freely Latinizes: (2) those who believe the Letters to be the work of Lucian. Here Boyle gives his reasons—excellent as far as they go—for holding that Lucian was *not* the author. He then resumes:

> "These are my reasons for not ascribing the Letters to Lucian; there are other reasons which make me doubt whether Phalaris can claim the Letters as his own. It was scarcely possible that Letters written by so distinguished a man, and in their own kind perfect, should have remained completely hidden for more than a thousand years: and, as Sicilian writers always preferred the Dorian dialect, the tyrant of the Agrigentines (who were Dorians) ought to have used no other. In the style there is nothing unworthy of a king, except that he is too fond of antithesis, and sometimes rather frigid. I have also noticed that sometimes (though that may be accidental) the Letters bear names which look as if they had been invented to suit the contents. As to history, time has robbed us of all certain knowledge regarding the state of Sicily and its commonwealth, in that age; and the recipients of the letters are mostly obscure, except Stesichorus, Pythagoras, and Abaris; whose age agrees with that of Phalaris—thus affording no hold for doubt on that ground. If, how-

ever, Diodorus Siculus is right in saying that Tauromenium, whose
citizens our author addresses, was built and so called after the destruction of Naxos by the younger Dionysius—then the claim of Phalaris is destroyed, and the whole fabric of conjectural ascription falls
to the ground. This is the sum of what I had to say on my author—
set forth, indeed, somewhat hastily; but, if more learned men have
anything to urge against it, I am ready to hear it."

Boyle wrote this, let it be remembered, before Bentley
had published anything on the subject. Boyle was strictly justified in saying afterwards, " I never profess'd myself
a patron of Phalaris ;" " I was not in the least concern'd
to vindicate the Letters." He defines his own position
with exactness in another place : " Phalaris was always a
favourite book with me: from the moment I knew it, I
wish'd it might prove an original : I had now and then,
indeed, some suspicions that 'twas not genuine; but I
lov'd him so much more than I suspected him, that I
wou'd not suffer myself to dwell long upon 'em. To be
sincere, the opinion, or mistake, if you will, was so pleasing
that I was somewhat afraid of being undeceiv'd." It was
Sir William Temple, not Boyle, who was committed to the
view that the Letters were genuine.

We shall speak of Bentley's Dissertation in its second
and mature form. The first rough draft, in Wotton's book,
is a rapid argument, with just enough illustration to make
each topic clear. It had been very hastily written. That
Boyle and his friends should have been angry, can surprise
no one. Bentley, in rebutting a calumny, had become a
rough assailant. A reply came out in January, 1696. It
was entitled, " Dr. Bentley's Dissertations on the Epistles
of Phalaris and the Fables of Æsop, examin'd by the Honourable Charles Boyle, Esq." The motto was taken from
Roscommon's " Essay of Translated Verse :"

"Remember Milo's end ;
Wedg'd in that Timber, which he strove to rend."

The piece is clever and effective. "Soon after Dr.
Bentley's Dissertation came out," Boyle says in the preface, "I was call'd away into Ireland, to attend the Parliament there. The publick business, and my own private
affairs, detain'd me a great while in that kingdom ; else
the world should have had a much earlier account of him
and his performance." Boyle explains that he had edited
the Letters "rather as one that wish'd well to learning
than profess'd it." His motive for replying to Bentley's
attack is "the publick affront" of being charged with setting his name to a book which was not his own. No one
had helped him in it—except one friend who had been his
adviser "upon any difficulty," and had also consulted "some
books" for him "in the Oxford Libraries." As to the
Letters, he had neither asserted nor denied their genuineness. He is sorry to have been the occasion of bringing
such a storm on the head of Sir William Temple. He regrets, too, that Bentley should have extended his asper-
sions to Christ Church. Then comes an onslaught on
Bentley's essay and a defence of Boyle's book. "A Short
Account of Dr. Bentley by way of Index" was appended
to the second edition. This is an index to the preceding
266 pages, under such heads as these : "Dr. Bentley's
Civil Usage of Mr. Boyle ; His Singular Humanity to
Mr. Boyle ; His Elegant Similes ; His Clean and Gentile
Metaphors ; His Old Sayings and Proverbs ; His Collection of Asinine Proverbs ; His Extraordinary Talent
at Drollery ; His Dogmatical Air ; His Ingenuity in
transcribing and plundering Notes and Prefaces of Mr.
Boyle [here follows a list of other victims]. His Mod-
esty and Decency in contradicting Great Men [here fol-

lows a list of the persons contradicted, ending with *Every-body*]."

This, we know, was a joint performance. Francis Atterbury, afterwards Bishop of Rochester, was then thirty-six: George Smalridge was a year younger. Both were already distinguished at Oxford. Atterbury, in a letter to Boyle, says with reference to this piece: "in writing more than half of the book, in reviewing a good part of the rest, in transcribing the whole and attending the press half a year of my life has passed away." Smalridge is supposed to have contributed a playful proof that Bentley did not write his own essay. This is a parody of Bentley's arguments about Phalaris, partly woven with his own words and phrases. This sham Bentley—urges the critic —"is a perfect Dorian in his language, in his thoughts, and in his breeding." It is vain to plead that "he was born in some Village remote from Town, and bred among the Peasantry while young." The real Bentley had been "a Member of one University, and a Sojourner in the other; a Chaplain in Ordinary to the King, and a Tutor in extra-ordinary to a Young Gentleman:" such a man must surely have written *Attic;* he must "have quitted his Old Country Dialect for that of a Londoner, a Gentleman, and a Scholar." Then the sham Bentley is "a Fierce and Angry Writer; and One, who when he thinks he has an advantage over another Man, gives him no Quarter." But the real Bentley says in his Letter to Dr. Mill, "it is not in my nature to trample upon the Prostrate." The real Bentley was "much vers'd in the Learned Languages." This pseudo-Bentley shows "that he was not only a perfect Stranger to the best Classic Authors, but that he wanted that Light which any Ordinary Dictionary would have afforded him." The pages on Æsop may have been

chiefly due to Anthony Alsop, a young Student of Christ
Church, who edited the Fables in that year (1698).   The
" very deserving gentleman " to whom Boyle refers as his
assistant appears to have been John Freind, whose brother
Robert (both were Students of Christ Church) is also believed to have helped.   Some of the insults to Bentley
are very gross.   Thus it is hinted, twice over, that his
further compliance in the mátter of the manuscript might
have been purchased by a fee.   This is the only thing in
the piece which Bentley noticed with a word of serious
reproof.

The book gives us some curious glimpses of the way in
which critical studies were then viewed by Persons of
Honour.   " Begging the Dr's pardon," says Boyle, " I take
Index-hunting after Words and Phrases to be, next after
Anagrams and *Acrosticks*, the lowest Diversion a Man can
betake himself to."   Boyle is apprehensive lest " worthy
Men, who know so well how to employ their hours, should
be diverted from the pursuit of Useful Knowledge into
such trivial Enquiries as these:" and he shrinks from being suspected of having " thrown away any considerable
part of his life on so trifling a subject."   He need not
have felt much uneasiness.

However small Boyle's share in this book may have
been, it is right to observe that there is an almost ludicrous exaggeration in the popular way of telling the story,
as if all Christ Church, or all Oxford, had been in a league
to annihilate Bentley.   The joint book was written by a
group of clever friends who represented only themselves.
Rymer, indeed, says, " Dr. Aldrich, no doubt, was at the
head of them, and smoaked and punned plentifully on
this occasion."   But this was a mistake.   The " Short
Review " published anonymously in 1701 (the author was

Atterbury) says expressly : "That an answer was preparing, he [the Dean of Christ Church] knew nothing of
till 'twas publick talk, and he never saw a line of the *Examination* but in Print."

In the preface to Anthony Alsop's Æsop—another of
the Christ Church editions, which came out, before
Boyle's book, early in 1698—our hero is mentioned as
"a certain Bentley, diligent enough in turning over lexicons ;" and his behaviour about the manuscript is indicated by a Latin version of "The Dog in the Manger."
The wearied ox, coming home to dinner, is driven from
his hay by the snarling usurper, and remonstrates warmly ; when the dog replies, "You call me currish ; if foreigners are any judges, there is not a hound alive that ap-
proaches me in humanity." To whom the ox : "Is this
your *singular humanity*, to refuse me the food that you
will not and cannot enjoy yourself ?"

At last "Boyle against Bentley" came out (1698). Its
success was enormous. A second edition was called for
in a few months. A third edition followed in the next
year. Forty-six years later, when both the combatants
were dead, it was still thought worth while to publish a
fourth edition.

Temple lost no time in pronouncing. In March, just
after the book appeared, he writes : "The compass and
application of so much learning, the strength and perti-
nence of his (Boyle's) arguments, the candour of his relations, in return to such foul-mouthed raillery, the pleasant turns of wit, and the easiness of style, are in my opinion as extraordinary as the contrary of these all appear to
be in what the Doctor and his friend [Wotton] have written." Hard as this is on Bentley, it is harder still on
poor Wotton, who had been elaborately civil to Temple.

Garth published his *Dispensary* in 1699, with that luckless couplet—meant, says Noble, "to please his brother wits at Button's:"

> "So diamonds take a lustre from their foil,
> And to a Bentley 'tis we owe a Boyle."

John Milner, formerly Vicar of Leeds, had, as a non-juror, lost his preferments at the Revolution, and was then living at St. John's College, Cambridge. In his "View of the Dissertation" (1698) he proposes "to manifest the incertitude of heathen chronology," and takes part against Bentley. According to Eustace Budgell, a caricature was published at Cambridge, in which Phalaris was consigning Bentley to the bull, while the Doctor exclaimed, "I would rather be roasted than boyled." Rymer, in his "Essay on Critical and Curious Learning" (1698), blames both parties. As to the question at issue, he argues that "curious" learning is all very well in its way, but should not be carried too far. On Boyle's critique Rymer makes a shrewd remark: "There is such a profusion of wit all along, and such variety of points and raillery, that every man seems to have thrown in a repartee or so in his turn." Mr. Cole (of Magdalen College, Oxford) compared it to "a Cheddar cheese, made of all the milk of the parish."

In short, "society" had declared against Bentley, and the men of letters almost unanimously agreed with it. While other acquaintances were turning their backs, Evelyn stood loyal. That was the state of things in 1698. Bentley remained calm. A friend who met him one day urged him not to lose heart. "Indeed," he replied, "I am in no pain about the matter; for it is a maxim with me that no man was ever written out of reputation but by himself." Meanwhile he was preparing a reply.

4

CHAPTER V.

WE have seen that Bentley's essay in Wotton's book had been a hasty production. "I drew up that dissertation," he says, "in the spare hours of a few weeks; and while the Printer was employed about one leaf, the other was amaking." He now set to work to revise and enlarge it. He began his task about March, 1698—soon after Boyle's pamphlet appeared—but was interrupted in it by the two months of his residence at Worcester, from the end of May to the end of July. It was finished toward the close of 1698. The time employed upon it had thus been about seven and a half months, not free from other and urgent duties. It was published early in 1699. Let us clearly apprehend the point at issue. Boyle did not assert that the Letters of Phalaris were genuine; but he denied that Bentley had yet proved them to be spurious.

After a detailed refutation of the personal charges against him, Bentley comes to the Letters of Phalaris. First he takes the flagrant anachronisms. The Letters mention towns which, at the supposed date, were not built, or bore other names. Phalaris presents his physician with the ware of a potter named Thericles—much as if Oliver Cromwell were found dispensing the masterpieces

of Wedgwood. Phalaris quotes books which had not been
written; nay, he is familiar with forms of literature which
had not been created.   Though a Dorian, he writes to his
familiar friends in Attic, and in a species of false Attic
which did not exist for five centuries after he was dead.
Farmer of the taxes though he had been, he has no idea
of values in the ordinary currency of his own country.
Thus he complains that the hostile community of Catana
had made a successful raid on his principality, and had
robbed him of no less a sum than seven talents. Again,
he mentions with some complacency that he has bestowed
the munificent dower of five talents on a lady of distinction.   According to the Sicilian standard, the loss of the
prince would have amounted to twelve shillings and seven
pence, while the noble bride would have received nine
shillings.   The occasions of the letters, too, are often singular.   A Syracusan sends his brother to Akragas, a distance of a hundred miles, with a request that Phalaris
would send a messenger to Stesichorus (another hundred
miles or so), and beg that poet to write a copy of verses
on the Syracusan's deceased wife.   "This," says Bentley,
"is a scene of putid and senseless formality."   Then Phalaris (who brags in one of the letters that Pythagoras had
stayed five months with him) says to Stesichorus, "*pray*
do not mention me in your poems."   "This," says Bentley, "was a sly fetch of our sophist, to prevent so shrewd
an objection from Stesichorus's silence as to any friendship at all with him."   But supposing Phalaris had really
been so modest—Bentley adds—still, Stesichorus was a
man of the world.   The poet would have known "that
those sort of requests are but a modest simulation, and a
disobedience would have been easily pardoned."   Again,
these Letters are not mentioned by any writer before the

fifth century of our era, and it is clear that the ancients
did not know them. Thus, in the Letters, Phalaris displays the greatest solicitude for the education of his son
Paurolas, and writes to the young man in terms which
would do credit to the best of fathers. But in Aristotle's
time there was a tradition which placed the parental conduct of Phalaris in another light. It alleged, in fact,
that, while this boy was still of a tender age, the prince
had caused him to be served up at table : but how, asks
Bentley—supposing the Letters to be genuine—" could he
eat his son while he was an infant ?" It is true, the works
of some writers in the early Christian centuries (Phædrus,
Paterculus, Lactantius) are not mentioned till long after
their death. But the interval was one during which the
Western world was lapsing into barbarism. The supposed
epoch of Phalaris was followed by " the greatest and longest
reign of learning that the world has yet seen :" and yet
his Letters remain hidden for a thousand years. " Take
them in the whole bulk, they are a fardle of common-
places, without any life or spirit from action and circumstance. Do but cast your eye upon Cicero's letters, or
any statesman's, as Phalaris was; what lively characters
of men there ! what descriptions of place ! what notifica-
tions of time ! what particularity of circumstances ! what
multiplicity of designs and events ! When you return to
these again, you feel, by the emptiness and deadness of
them, that you converse with some dreaming pedant with
his elbow on his desk ; not with an active, ambitious tyrant, with his hand on his sword, commanding a million
of subjects."

Bentley's incidental discussions of several topics are so
many concise monographs, each complete in itself, each
exhaustive within its own limits, and each, at the same

time, filling its due place in the economy of the whole.
Such are the essays on the age of Pythagoras, on the be-
ginnings of Greek Tragedy, on anapæstic verse, on the
coinage of Sicily. In the last-named subject, it might
have appeared almost impossible that a writer of Bentley's
time should have made any near approximation to correctness. He had not such material aids as are afforded by
the Sicilian coins which we now possess—without which
the statements of ancient writers would appear involved in
hopeless contradiction. I am glad, therefore, to quote an
estimate of Bentley's work in this department by a master
of numismatic science. Mr. Barclay Head writes: "Speaking generally, Bentley's results are surprisingly accurate. I
think I may safely say that putting aside what was to have
been done within the last fifty years, Bentley's essay stands
alone. Even Eckhel, in his 'Doctrina numorum' (1790),
has nothing to compare with it." Again, Bentley's range
and grasp of knowledge are strikingly seen in critical remarks of general bearing which are drawn from him by
the course of the discussion. Thus at the outset he gives
in a few words a broad view of the origin and growth of
literary forgery in the ancient world. In the last two
centuries before Christ, when there was a keen rivalry between the libraries of Pergamus and Alexandria, the copi-
ers of manuscripts began the practice of inscribing them
with the names of great writers, in order that they might
fetch higher prices. Thus far, the motive of falsification
was simply mercenary. But presently a different cause
began to swell the number of spurious works. It was a
favourite exercise of rhetoric, in the early period of the
Empire, to compose speeches or letters in the name and
character of some famous person. At first such exercises
would, of course, make no pretence of being anything

more. But, as the art was developed, "some of the Greek
Sophists had the success and satisfaction to see their essays in that kind pass with some readers for the genuine
works of those they endeavoured to express. This, no
doubt, was great content and joy to them ; being as full a
testimony of their skill in imitation, as the birds gave to
the painter when they pecked at his grapes." Some of
them, indeed, candidly confessed the trick. "But most
of them took the other way, and, concealing their own
names, put off their copies for originals ; preferring that
silent pride and fraudulent pleasure, though it was to die
with them, before an honest commendation from posterity
for being good imitators." And hence such Letters as
those of Phalaris.

Dr. Aldrich had lately dedicated his Logic to Charles
Boyle. Bentley makes a characteristic use of this circumstance. "If his new System of Logic teaches him
such arguments," says Bentley, "I'll be content with the
old ones." The whole Dissertation, in fact, is a remorse-
less syllogism. But Bentley is more than a sound rea-
soner. He shows in a high degree the faculties which
go to make debating power. He is frequently successful in the useful art of turning the tables. Alluding to
his opponent's mock proof that "Dr. Bentley could not
be the author of the Dissertation," he remarks that Boyle's
Examination is open to a like doubt in good earnest, if we
are to argue "from the variety of styles in it, from its
contradictions to his edition of Phalaris, from its contradictions to itself, from its contradictions to Mr. B.'s
character and to his title of honourable." Boyle had said
of Bentley, "the man that writ this must have been fast
asleep, for else he could never have talked so wildly."
Bentley replies, "I hear a greater paradox talked of

abroad; that not the 'wild' only, but the best, part of
the Examiner's book may possibly have been written
while he was fast asleep."

He is often neat, too, in exploding logical fallacies.
Boyle argued that, as Diodorus gives two different dates
for the founding of Tauromenium, neither can be trusted.
Bentley rejoins: "One man told me in company that the
Examiner was twenty-four years old; and another said,
twenty-five. Now, these two stories contradict one another, and neither can be depended on; we are at liberty,
therefore, to believe him a person of about fifty years of
age." Boyle had taken refuge in a desperate suggestion
that people might have been called "Tauromenites" from a
river Tauromenius, before there was a city Tauromenium.
"Now," says Bentley, "if the Tauromenites were a sort
of fish, this argument drawn from the river would be of
great force." Boyle had argued that a Greek phrase was
not poetical because each of the two words forming it
was common. Bentley quotes from Lucretius:

"Luna dies, et nox, et noctis signa severa."

Is not every word common? And is the total effect pro-
saic? Bentley's retort is a mere quibble, turning on the
ambiguity of "common" as meaning either "vulgar" or
"simple"—but illustrates his readiness. Once—as if in
contempt for his adversary's understanding—he has in-
dulged in a notable sophism. Boyle had argued that the
name "tragedy" cannot have existed before the *thing*.
Bentley rejoins: "'tis a proposition false in itself *that
things themselves must be, before the names by which they
are called*. For we have many new tunes in music made
every day, which never existed before; yet several of
them are called by *names* that were formerly in use; and

perhaps the tune of Chevy Chase, though it be of famous antiquity, is a little younger than the name of the chase itself. And I humbly conceive that Mr. Hobbes's book, which he called the *Leviathan*, is not quite as ancient as its name is in Hebrew." But the "name" of which Boyle spoke was descriptive, not merely appellative. Bentley's reasoning would have been relevant only if Boyle had argued that, since a tragedy is called the "Agamemnon," Tragedy must have existed before Agamemnon lived.

As to the English style of the Dissertation, the Boyle party had expressed their opinion pretty freely when the first draft of it had appeared in Wotton's book. They complained that, when Bentley "had occasion to express himself in Terms of Archness and Waggery," he descended to "low and mean Ways of Speech." "The familiar expressions of *taking one tripping — coming off with a whole skin, minding his hits — a friend at a pinch — going to blows — setting horses together*—and *going to pot;* with others borrow'd from the Sports and Employments of the Country; shew our Author to have been accustom'd to another sort of Exercise than that of the Schools." Alluding to the painful fate which was said to have overtaken the mother of Phalaris, Bentley particularly shocked his critics by the phrase, "Roasting the old Woman;" and, in a similar strain of rustic levity, he had described the parent of Euripides as "Mother Clito the Herbwoman." Dr. King, of Christ Church (who, it will be remembered, had meddled in the manuscript affair), had written an account of a journey to London; wherein he relates that, on his asking concerning the ales at a certain inn, the host answered "that he had a thousand such sort of liquors, as humtie dumtie, three-threads, four-threads, old Pharoah [*sic*], knockdown, hugmetee," &c. Playfully re-

ferring to this passage, Bentley says (speaking of a wild
assertion), " A man must be dosed with Humty - dumty
that could talk so inconsistently ;" and again, speaking of
Dr. King's statements, " If he comes with more testimonies of his Bookseller or his Humty-dumty acquaintance,
I shall take those for no answer." Worst of all, this familiar style was used towards Phalaris himself and his
defenders. Speaking of the Greek rhetoricians, Bentley
announces that his design is "to pull off the disguise from
those little Pedants that have so long stalkt about in the
Apparel of Heroes." The work of Boyle and his assistants is thus characterised : "Here are your Work-men to
mend an author ; as bungling Tinkers do old kettles ;
there was but one hole in the text before they meddled
with it, but they leave it with two."

Not a soothing style this, nor one to be recommended
for imitation. But what vigour there is in some of the
phrases that Bentley strikes out at a red heat! They
ought to have made inquiries "before they ventur'd to
Print—*which is a sword in the hand of a Child.*" "He
gives us some shining metaphors, and a polished period or
two; but, for the matter of it, it is *some common and obvious thought dressed and curled in the beauish way.*"
Speaking of work which Bishop Pearson had left unfin-
ished : "though it has not passed the last hand of the
author, yet it's every way worthy of him ; and the *very
dust of his writings is gold.*" And here—as Bentley was
charged in this controversy with such boundless arrogance,
and such "indecency in contradicting great men"—let us
note his tone in the Dissertation towards eminent men
then living or lately dead. Nothing could be more becoming, more worthy of his own genius, than the warm, often
glowing, terms in which he speaks of such men as Selden,

4*

Pearson, Lloyd, Stillingfleet, Spanheim—in a word, of almost all the distinguished scholars whom he has occasion to name. Dodwell, who was ranged against him, is treated with scrupulous courtesy and fairness. Joshua Barnes, whose own conduct to Bentley had been remarkably bad, could scarcely be described more indulgently than in these words—"one of a singular industry and a most diffuse reading." Those were precisely the two things which could truly be said in praise of Barnes, and it would not have been easy to find a third.

Hallam characterises the style of the Dissertation as "rapid, concise, amusing, and superior to Boyle in that which he had chiefly to boast, a sarcastic wit." It may be questioned how far "wit," in its special modern sense, was a distinguishing trait on either side of this controversy. The chief weapons of the Boyle alliance were rather derision and invective. Bentley's sarcasm is always powerful and often keen; but the finer quality of wit, though seen in some touches, can hardly be said to pervade the Dissertation. As to the humour, that is unquestionable. There is so far an unconscious element in it, that its effect on the reader is partly due to Bentley's tremendous and unflagging earnestness in heaping up one absurdity upon another. This cumulative humour belongs to the essay as a whole; as Bentley marches on triumphantly from one exposure to another, our sense of the ludicrous is constantly rising. But it can be seen on a smaller scale too. For instance, one of Boyle's grievances was that Bentley had indirectly called him an ass. In Bentley's words: "By the help, he says, of a Greek proverb, I call him a downright ass. After I had censured a passage of Mr. Boyle's translation that has no affinity with the original, *This puts me in mind*, said I, *of the old Greek proverb, that Leucon carries one*

thing, and his Ass quite another.　Where the Ass is manifestly spoken of the Sophist [the real author of the Let-
ters], whom I had before represented as *an Ass under a
Lion's skin.*　And if Mr. B. has such a dearness for his
Phalaris that he'll change places with him there, how can
I help it?　I can only protest that I put him into Leucon's
place; and if he will needs compliment himself out of it,
'*I must leave the two friends to the pleasure of their mutual
civilities.*'"　[Boyle's own words about Bentley and Wotton.]　But this was not all: Boyle had accused Bentley
of comparing him to *Lucian's* ass.　Now this, says Bentley, "were it true, would be no coarse compliment, but a
very obliging one.　For Lucian's Ass was a very intelligent and ingenious Ass, and had more sense than any of
his Riders; he was no other than Lucian himself in the
shape of an ass, and had a better talent at kicking and
bantering than ever the Examiner will have, though it
seems to be his chief one."　"But is this Mr. B.'s way of
interpreting similitudes? . . . If I liken an ill critic to a
bungling Tinker, that makes two holes while he mends
one; must I be charged with calling him Tinker?　At
this rate Homer will call his heroes Wolves, Boars, Dogs,
and Bulls.　And when Horace has this comparison about
himself,

'Demitto auriculas, ut iniquae mentis asellus,'

Mr. B. may tell him that he calls himself downright ass.
But he must be put in mind of the English proverb, that
similitudes, even when they are taken from asses, do not
walk upon all four."　Swift—alluding to the transference
of the Letters from Phalaris to their real source—called
Bentley that "great rectifier of saddles."　Bentley might
have replied that he could rectify panniers too.

It would be a mistake to regard Bentley's Dissertation as if its distinctive merit had consisted in demonstrating the Letters of Phalaris to be spurious. That was by no means Bentley's own view. The spuriousness of these Letters, he felt from the first, was patent. He had given (in Wotton's book) a few of the most striking proofs of this: and he had been attacked. Now he was showing, in self-defence, that his proofs not only held good, but had deep and solid foundations. Others before him had suspected that the letters were forgeries, and he would have scorned to take the smallest credit for seeing what was so plain. He was the first to give sufficient reasons for his belief; but he did not care, and did not pretend, to give all the reasons that might be adduced. Indeed, any careful reader of the Letters can remark several proofs of spuriousness on which Bentley has not touched. For instance, it could be shown that the fictitious proper names are post-classical; that the forger was acquainted with Thucydides; and that he had read the *Theætetus* of Plato. But Bentley had done more than enough for his purpose. The glory of his treatise was not that it established his conclusion, but that it disclosed that broad and massive structure of learning upon which his conclusion rested. "The only book that I have writ upon my own account," he says, "is this present answer to Mr. B.'s objections; and I assure him I set no great price upon 't; the errors that it refutes are so many, so gross and palpable, that I shall never be very proud of the victory." At the same time, he justly refutes the assertion of his adversaries that the point at issue was of no moment. Bentley replies: "That the single point whether Phalaris be genuine or no is of no small importance to learning, the very learned Mr. Dodwell is a sufficient evidence; who, espous-

ing Phalaris for a true author, has endeavoured by that
means to make a great innovation in the ancient chronology. To undervalue this dispute about Phalaris because
it does not suit to one's own studies, is to quarrel with a
circle because it is not a square."

A curious fatality attended on Bentley's adversaries in
this controversy.   While they dealt thrusts at points
where he was invulnerable, they missed all the chinks in
his armour except a statement limiting too narrowly the
use of two Greek verbs, and his identification of "Alba
Graeca" with Buda instead of Belgrade. Small and few,
indeed, these chinks were. It would have been a petty,
but fair, triumph for his opponents, if they had perceived
that, in correcting a passage of Aristophanes, he had left a
false quantity.   They might have shown that a passage in
Diodorus had led him into an error regarding Attic chronology during the reign of the Thirty Tyrants   They
might have exulted in the fact that an emendation which
he proposed in Isæus rested on a confusion between two
different classes of choruses; that he had certainly mis-
construed a passage in the life of Pythagoras by Iambli-
chus; that the "Minos," on which he relies as Plato's
work, was spurious; that, in one of the Letters of Phalaris, he had defended a false reading by false grammar.
They could have shown that Bentley was demonstrably
wrong in asserting that no writings, bearing the name of
Æsop, were extant in the time of Aristophanes; also in
stating that the Fable of "The Two Boys" had not
come down to the modern world: it was, in fact, very
near them—safe in a manuscript at the Bodleian Library.   Even the discussion on Zaleucus escaped: its weak
points were first brought out by later critics — Warburton, Salter, Gibbon. Had such blemishes been ten times

more numerous, they would not have affected the worth
of the book; but, such as they were, they were just of
the kind which small detractors delight to magnify.   In
one place Bentley accuses Boyle of having adopted a
wrong reading in one of the Letters, and thereby made
nonsense of the passage.   Now, Boyle's reading, though
not the best, happens to be capable of yielding the very
sense which Bentley required.   Yet even this Boyle and
his friends did not discover.

How was the Dissertation received?   According to the
popular account, no sooner had Bentley blown his mighty
blast, than the walls of the hostile fortress fell flat.   The
victory was immediate, the applause universal, the foe's ruin
overwhelming.   Tyrwhitt, in his *Babrius*—published long
after Bentley's death—is seeking to explain why Bentley
never revised the remarks on Æsop, which he had published in Wotton's book.   "Content with having pros-
trated his adversaries with the second Dissertation on
Phalaris, as by a thunder-bolt, he withdrew in scorn from
the uneven fight."

Let us see what the evidence is.   Just as the great Dissertation appeared, Boyle's friends published "A short Account of Dr. Bentley's Humanity and Justice."   It is conceived in a rancorous spirit; Bentley is accused of having
plundered, in his Fragments of Callimachus, some papers
which Thomas Stanley, the editor of Æschylus, left unpublished at his death; and Bentley's conduct to Boyle
about the manuscript is set forth as related by the bookseller, Mr. Bennet.   Now, in John Locke's correspondence,
I find a letter to him from Thomas Burnet, formerly a
Fellow of Christ's College, Cambridge, and then Master of
Charterhouse, author of a fantastic book on the geological
history of the earth (*Telluris Theoria Sacra*).   The date

is March 19, 1699. Bentley had read part of his preface to Burnet before it was published. Burnet had now read the whole, and a great part of the Dissertation itself; also the newly published "Short Account." He is now disposed to believe Bennet's version. "I do profess, upon second thoughts . . . that his story seemeth the more likely, if not the most true, of the two." As to the Letters of Phalaris, he is aware that some great scholars are with Bentley. "But I doubt not," he adds, "that a greater number will be of another sentiment, who would not be thought to be of the unlearned tribe." That, we may be sure, was what many people were saying in London. A defence of Bentley against the "Short Account," which came out at this time, has been ascribed to a Fellow of Magdalen College, Oxford — Solomon Whately, the first translator of Phalaris into English.

The Boyle party had addressed themselves to the wits and the town. Bentley's work had plenty of qualities which could be appreciated in that quarter; but its peculiar strength lay in things of which few persons could judge. These few were at once convinced by it; and their authority helped to convince the inner circles of students. But the Boyle party still had on their side all those who, regarding the contest as essentially an affair of style, preferred Boyle's style to Bentley's. This number would include the rank and file of fashion and its dependents—the persons who wrote dedications, and the patrons in whose antechambers they waited. Most of them would be genuinely unconscious how good Bentley's answer was, and their prepossessions would set strongly the other way. So, while Bentley had persuaded the scholars, it would still be the tone of a large and influential world to say that, though the pedant might have brought cumbrous proofs of a few trivial points, Boyle had won a signal victory in "wit, taste, and breeding."

Swift's "Battle of the Books" was begun when he was living with Sir William Temple at Moor Park in 1697. It was suggested by a French satire, Coutray's *Histoire Poétique de la guerre nouvellement déclarée entre les anciens et les modernes*, and referred to Bentley's *first* Dissertation, which had just appeared. Temple was feeling sore, and Swift wished to please him. But its circulation was only private until it was published with the "Tale of a Tub" in 1704. Temple had then been dead five years. If Bentley's victory had then been universally recognised as crushing, Swift would have been running the risk of turning the laugh against himself; and no man, so fond of wounding, liked that less. In the "Battle of the Books," Boyle is Achilles, clad in armour wrought by the gods. The character ascribed to Bentley and Wotton is expressed in the Homeric similes which adorn the grand battle at the end. "As a Woman in a little House, that gets a painful livelihood by spinning; if chance her Geese be scattered o'er the Common, she courses round the plain from side to side, compelling, here and there, the stragglers to the flock; they cackle loud, and flutter o'er the champain: so Boyle pursued, so fled this Pair of Friends. . . . As when a skilful Cook has truss'd a brace of Woodcocks, he, with iron Skewer, pierces the tender sides of both, their legs and wings close pinion'd to their ribs; so was this Pair of Friends transfix'd, till down they fell, join'd in their lives, join'd in their deaths; so closely join'd that Charon would mistake them both for one, and waft them over Styx for half his fare." When this was first published, Bentley's second Dissertation had been five years before the public.

Against this satire—so purely popular that it lost nothing by being whetted on the wrong edge—we must set two pieces of contemporary evidence to Bentley's immediate success with his own limited audience. In discussing the age of Pythagoras, he had said: "I do not pretend to pass my own judgment, or to determine positively on either side; but I submit the whole to the censure of such readers as are well versed in ancient learning; and particularly to that incomparable historian and chronologer, the Right Reverend the Bishop of Coventry and Litchfield." In the same year (1699) Dr. Lloyd responded by publishing his views on the question, prefaced by a dedicatory epistle to Bentley. The other testimony is of a different kind, but not less significant. "A Short Review" of the controversy appeared in 1701. It was anonymous. Dyce says that a friend of his possessed a copy in which an early eighteenth century hand had written, "by Dr. Atterbury." The internal evidence leaves no doubt of this. I may notice one indication of it, which does not appear to have been remarked. We have seen that the "Examination" of Bentley's first essay was edited, and in great part written, by Atterbury. This ends with these words: "I fancy that the reader will be glad to have . . . the Dr.'s Picture in Miniature," rather "than that it shou'd be again drawn out *at full length*." The "picture in miniature" is the "Index" already mentioned above. Now the "Short Review" ends with "the Dr.'s Advantagious Character of himself *at full length*." The writer of this "Character" is clearly going back on his own footsteps: and that writer can be no other than Atterbury. He is very angry, and intensely bitter. He hints that Whig interest has bolstered up Bentley against Tory opponents. With almost incredible violence, he accuses Bentley of "lying, stealing, and prevaricating" (p. 12). He contrasts the character of a "Critic" with that of a "Gentleman." Stress is laid on the imputation that Bentley had attacked not Boyle alone, but also the illustrious society in which Boyle had been educated. The members of that society (Atterbury remarks) are not cut all alike, as Bushels are by Winchester-measure: "But they are men of different Talents, Principles, Humours, and Interests, who are seldom or never united save when some unreasonable oppression from abroad fastens them together, and consequently whatever ill is said of all of them is falsely said of many of them." "To answer the reflexion of a private Gentleman with a general abuse of the Society he belong'd to, is the manners of a dirty Boy upon a Country-Green." It will not avail Bentley that his friends "style him a Living Library, a Walking Dictionary, and a Constellation of Criticism." A solitary gleam of humour varies this strain. Some wiseacre had suggested that the Letters of Phalaris might corrupt the crowned heads of Europe, if kings should take up the Agrigentine tyrant as Alexander the Great took up Homer, and put him under their pillows at night. "I objected"—says the author of the "Short Review"— "that now, since the advancement of Learning and Civility in the world, Princes were more refined, and would be ashamed of such acts of Barbarity as Phalaris was guilty of in a ruder age." But the alarmist stuck to his point; urging that "his Czarish Majesty" (Peter the Great, then in the twelfth year of his reign) might have met with the Letters of Phalaris in his travels, and that "his curiosity might have led him to make a Brazen Bull, when he came home, to burn his Rebells in." The piece ends by renewing the charge of plagiarism against Bent-

ley. Considering that the second Dissertation had now
been out two years, this is a curiosity of literature:
"*Common Pilferers will still go on in their trade, even
after they have suffer'd for it.*"

But, when Bentley's Dissertation had been published
for half a century, surely there can have been no longer
any doubt as to the completeness of his victory? We
shall see. In 1749, seven years after Bentley's death, an
English Translation of the Letters of Phalaris was published by Thomas Francklin. He had been educated at
Westminster School, and was then a resident Fellow of
Trinity College, Cambridge; his translation of Sophocles
is still well known. He dedicates his version of Phalaris
to John, Earl of Orrery, alluding to the esteem in which
the Greek author had been held by the late Lord Orrery
(Charles Boyle). He then refers to "the celebrated dispute" between Boyle and Dentley about these Letters.
"Doctor Bentley," he allows, "was always look'd on as
a man of wit and parts." On the other hand, Francklin
vindicates Boyle against "the foolish opinion" that he
had been helped by "some men of distinguished merit"
in his book against Bentley. Had this been so, those
men would have been eager to claim their share in the
reputation acquired by it. As they have not done so,
there can be no reason why Boyle's "claim to the deserved applause it has met with should ever for the future
be call'd in question." "I have not enter'd into any of
the points of the controversy," Francklin proceeds, "as it
would be a disagreeable as well as unnecessary task, but
shall only observe that, tho' *several very specious arguments are brought by Doctor Bentley, the strongest of them
do only affect particular epistles; which, as Mr. Boyle observes, do not hurt the whole body;* for in a collection

of pieces that have no dependence on each other, as epistles, epigrams, fables, the first number may be encreased
by the wantonness and vanity of imitators in aftertimes,
and *yet the book be authentic in the main, and an original
still.*"

Francklin was not outraging the sense of a learned
community by writing thus. In the very next year (1750)
he was elected to the Regius Professorship of Greek.
Nothing could show more conclusively the average state
of literary opinion on the controversy half a century after
it took place. But there is evidence which carries us fifty
years lower still. In 1804 Cumberland, Bentley's grandson, was writing his *Memoirs.* "I got together" (he
says) "all the tracts relative to the controversy between
Boyle and Bentley, omitting none even of the authorities
and passages they referred to, and having done this, I
compressed the reasonings on both sides into a kind of
statement and report upon the question in dispute; and
if, in the result, my judgment went with him to whom
my inclination lent, *no learned critic in the present age* will
condemn me for the decision." Such was the apologetic
tone which Bentley's grandson still thought due to the
world, even after Tyrwhitt had written of the "thunder-
bolt," and Porson of the "immortal Dissertation!" The
theory that Bentley had an immediate triumph does not
represent the general impression of his own age, but reflects the later belief of critical scholars, who felt the
crushing power of Bentley's reply, and imagined that
every one must have felt it when it first appeared. The
tamer account of the matter, besides being the truer, is
also far more really interesting. It shows how long the
clearest truth may have to wait.

Bentley's Dissertation was translated into Latin by the

Dutch scholar, John Daniel Lennep, who edited the Letters of Phalaris. After Lennep's death, the translation and the edition were published together by Valckenaer (1777). The Dissertation was subsequently rendered into German, with notes, by Ribbeck; and only seven years ago (1874) the English text of the Dissertation (both in its first and in its second form) was re-issued in Germany, with Introduction and notes, by Dr. Wilhelm Wagner. It has thus been the destiny of Bentley's work, truly a work of genius, to become in the best sense monumental. In a literature of which continual supersession is the law, it has owed this permanent place to its triple character as a storehouse of erudition, an example of method, and a masterpiece of controversy. Isaac Disraeli justly said of it that "it heaves with the workings of a master spirit." Bentley's learning everywhere bears the stamp of an original mind; and, even where it can be corrected by modern lights, has the lasting interest of showing the process by which an intellect of rare acuteness reached approximately true conclusions. As a consecutive argument it represents the first sustained application of strict reasoning to questions of ancient literature—a domain in which his adversaries, echoing the sentiment of their day, declared that "all is but a lucky guess." As a controversial reply, it is little less than marvellous, if we remember that his very clever assailants had been unscrupulous in their choice of weapons—freely using every sort of insinuation, however irrelevant or gross, which could tell—and that Bentley repulsed them at every point, without once violating the usages of legitimate warfare. While he demolishes, one by one, the whole series of their relevant remarks, he steadily preserves his own dignity by simply turning back upon them the dishonour of their own calumnies and the ridicule of their own impertinence.

With a dexterity akin to that of a consummate debater,
he wields the power of retort in such a manner that he
appears to be hardly more than the amused spectator of a
logical recoil.

Shortly before Swift described Boyle as Achilles, poor
Achilles was writing from Ireland, in some perturbation of
spirit, to those gods who were hard at work on his armour,
and confiding his hopes " that it would do no harm." It
did not do much. This was the first controversy in English letters that had made anything like a public stir, and
it is pleasant to think that Achilles and his antagonist appear to have been good friends afterwards : if any ill-will
lingered, it was rather in the bosoms of the Myrmidons.
Dr. William King, who had helped to make the mischief,
never forgave Bentley for his allusions to " Humty-dumty," and satirised him in ten "Dialogues of the Dead"
(on Lucian's model)—a title which suits their dulness.
Bentley is Bentivoglio, a critic who knows that the first
weather-cock was set up by the Argonauts and that cush-
ions were invented by Sardanapalus. Salter mentions a
tradition, current in 1777, that Boyle, after he became
Lord Orrery, visited Bentley at Trinity College, Cambridge. There is contemporary evidence, not, indeed, for
such personal intercourse, but for the existence of mutual
esteem. In 1721 a weekly paper, *The Spy*, attacked
Bentley in an article mainly patched up out of thefts
from Boyle's book on Phalaris, and a reply appeared, called " The Apothecary's Defence of Dr. Bentley, in answer
to the Spy." "Let me now tell it the Spy as a secret,"
says the Apothecary, " that Dr. Bentley has the greatest
deference for his noble antagonist (Boyle), both as a person of eminent parts and quality ; and I dare say his noble
antagonist thinks of Dr. Bentley as of a person as great

in critical learning as England has boasted of for many a
century." We remember Bentley's description of Boyle
as " a young gentleman of great hopes," and gladly believe
that the Apothecary was as well informed as his tone
would imply. Atterbury was in later life on excellent
terms with Bentley.

It is long enough now since " the sprinkling of a little
dust " allayed the last throb of angry passion that had
been roused by the Battle of the Books : but we look back
across the years, and see more than the persons of the
quarrel ; it was the beginning of a new epoch in criticism ;
and it is marked by a work which, to this hour, is classical
in a twofold sense, in relation to the literature of England
and to the philology of Europe.

CHAPTER VI.

Towards the end of 1699, about eight months after the
publication of Bentley's Dissertation on Phalaris, the Mastership of Trinity College, Cambridge, became vacant by
the removal of Dr. Mountague to the Deanery of Durham.
The nomination of a successor rested with six Commissioners, to whom King William had entrusted the duty of ad-
vising in the ecclesiastical and academic patronage of the
Crown. They were Archbishops Tenison and Sharp, with
Bishops Lloyd, Burnet, Patrick, and Moore — the last-
named in place of Stillingfleet, who had died in April,
1699. On their unanimous recommendation, the post
was given to Bentley. He continued to hold the office
of King's Librarian; but his home thenceforth was at
Cambridge.

No places in England have suffered so little as Oxford
and Cambridge from the causes which tend to merge local
colour in a monochrome. The academic world which
Bentley entered is still, after a hundred and eighty years,
comparatively near to us, both in form and in spirit. The
visitor in 1700, whom the coach conveyed in twelve hours
from the " Bull " in Bishopsgate Street to the " Rose " in
the Market-place of Cambridge, found a scene of which the

essential features were the same as they are to-day. The most distinctive among the older buildings of the University had long been such as we now see them; already for nearly two centuries the chapel of King's College had been standing in the completeness of its majestic beauty; the charm of the past could already be felt in the quadrangles and cloisters of many an ancient house, in pleasant shades and smooth lawns by the quiet river, in gardens with margins of bright flowers bordering time-stained walls, over which the sound of bells from old towers came like an echo of the middle age, in all the haunts which tradition linked with domestic memories of cherished names. It was only the environment of the University that was decidedly unlike the present. In the narrow streets of the little town, where feeble oil-lamps flickered at night, the projecting upper stories of the houses on either side approached each other so nearly overhead as partly to supply the place of umbrellas. The few shops that existed were chiefly open booths, with the goods displayed on a board which also served as a shutter to close the front. That great wilderness of peat-moss which once stretched from Cambridge to the Wash had not yet been drained with the thoroughness which has since reclaimed two thousand square miles of the best corn-land in England; tracts of fen still touched the outskirts of the town; snipe and marsh-fowl were plentiful in the present suburbs. To the south and south-east the country was unenclosed, as it remained, in great measure, down to the beginning of this century. A horseman might ride for miles without seeing a fence.

The broadest difference between the University life of Bentley's time and of our own might perhaps be roughly described by saying that, for the older men, it had more

5

resemblance, both in its rigours and in its laxities, to the
life of a monastery, and, for the younger men, to the life
of a school. The College day began with morning chapel,
usually at six. Breakfast was not a regular meal, but,
from about 1700, it was often taken at a coffee-house
where the London newspapers could be read. Morning
lectures began at seven or eight in the College hall.
Tables were set apart for different subjects. At "the
logick table" one lecturer is expounding Duncan's treatise, while another, at "the ethick table," is interpreting
Puffendorf on the Duty of a Man and a Citizen; classics
and mathematics engage other groups. The usual College
dinner-hour, which had long been 11 A.M., had advanced
before 1720 to noon. The afternoon disputations in the
Schools often drew large audiences to hear "respondent"
and "opponent" discuss such themes as "Natural Philosophy does not tend to atheism," or "Matter cannot
think." Evening chapel was usually at five; a slight
supper was provided in hall at seven or eight; and at
eight in winter, or nine in summer, the College gates
were locked. All students lodged within College walls.
Some tutors held evening lectures in their rooms. Discipline was stern. The birch-rod which was still hung up
at the butteries typified a power in the College dean similar to that which the fasces announced in the Roman Consul; and far on in the seventeenth century it was sometimes found to be more than an austere symbol, when a
youth showed himself, as Anthony Wood has it, "too
forward, pragmatic, and conceited." Boating, in the ath-
letic sense, was hardly known till about 1820, and the first
record of cricket in its present form is said to be the
match of Kent against England in 1746; but the undergraduates of Bentley's day played tennis, racquets, and

bowls; they rang peals on church-bells; they gave concerts; nay, we hear that the votaries " of Handel and Corelli " (the Italian violinist) were not less earnest than those of Newton and Locke. In Bentley's Cambridge the sense of a corporate life was strengthened by continuous residence. Many Fellows of Colleges, and some undergraduates, never left the University from one year's end to another. An excursion to the Bath or to Epsom Wells was the equivalent of a modern vacation-tour. No reading-party had yet penetrated to the Lakes or the Highlands. No summer fêtes yet brought an influx of guests; the nearest approach to anything of the kind was the annual Sturbridge Fair in September, held in fields near the Cam, just outside the town. The seclusion of the University world is curiously illustrated by the humorous speeches which old custom allowed on certain public occasions. The sallies of the academic satirist were to the Cambridge of that period very much what the Old Comedy was for the Athens of Aristophanes. The citizens of a compact commonwealth could be sufficiently entertained by lively criticism of domestic affairs, or by pointed allusions to the conduct of familiar persons.

In relation to the studies of Cambridge the moment of Bentley's arrival was singularly opportune. The theories of Descartes had just been exploded by that Newtonian philosophy which Bentley's Boyle Lectures had first popularised; in alliance with Newton's principles, a mathematical school was growing; and other sciences also were beginning to flourish. Between 1702 and 1727 the University was provided with chairs of Astronomy, Anatomy, Geology, and Botany; whilst the academic study of Medicine was also placed on a better footing. George I. founded the chair of Modern History in 1724. For classical

learning the latter part of the seventeenth century had
been a somewhat sterile period. There was thus a twofold function for a man of comprehensive vigour, holding
an eminent station in the University—to foster the new
learning, and to reanimate the old. Bentley proved himself equal to both tasks.

On February 1, 1700, the Fellows of Trinity College
met in the chapel for the purpose of admitting their
new Master. Bentley took the Latin oath, promising
(amongst other undertakings) that he would " observe
in all things the Statutes of the College, and interpret
them truly, sincerely, and according to their grammatical
sense;" that he would " rule and protect all and singular
Fellows and Scholars, Pensioners, Sizars, Subsizars, and
the other members of the College, according to the same
Statutes and Laws, without respect of birth, condition, or
person, without favour or ill-will;" that, in the event of
his resigning or being deposed, he would restore all that
was due to the College " without controversy or tergiver-
sation." He was then installed in the Master's seat, and
his reign began.

Bentley had just completed his thirty-eighth year. He
had a genius for scholarship, which was already recognised. He had also that which does not always accom-
pany it, a large enthusiasm for the advancement of learning. His powers of work were extraordinary, and his
physical strength was equal to almost any demand which
even he could make upon it. Seldom has a man of equal
gifts been placed at so early an age in a station which
offered such opportunities.

Henry VIII. founded Trinity College only a few weeks
before his death. Two establishments, each more than
two centuries old, then stood on the site of the present

Great Court.   One of these was Michael-house, founded in 1324 by Hervey de Stanton, Chancellor to Edward II. The other, King's Hall, was founded in 1337 by Edward III., who assigned it to the King's Scholars, thirty or forty students, maintained at Cambridge by a royal bounty, first granted by Edward II. in 1316.   Thus, whilst Michael-house was the older College, King's Hall represented the older foundation.   When Henry VIII. united them, the new name, "Trinity College," was probably taken from Michael-house, which, among other titles, had been dedicated to the Holy and Undivided Trinity.   The Reformation had been a crisis in the history of the English Universities.   In 1546 their fortunes were almost at the lowest ebb.   That fact adds significance to the terms in which Henry's charter traces the noble plan of Trinity College.   The new house is to be a "college of literature, the sciences, philosophy, good arts, and sacred Theology." It is founded "to the glory and honour of Almighty God and the Holy and Undivided Trinity; for the amplification and establishment of the Christian faith; the extirpation of heresy and false opinion; the increase and continuance of Divine Learning and all kinds of good letters; the knowledge of the tongues; the education of youth in piety, virtue, learning, and science; the relief of the poor, destitute, and afflicted; the prosperity of the Church of Christ; and the common good of his kingdom and subjects."

The King had died before this conception could be embodied in legislative enactment.   Statutes were made for Trinity College in the reign of Edward VI., and again in the reign of Mary.   Manuscript copies of these are preserved in the Muniment-room of the College; but the first printed code of Statutes was that given in the second year of Elizabeth. These governed Trinity College until a revision produced the "Victorian" Statutes of 1844. Two features of the Elizabethan Statutes deserve notice. All the sixty Fellowships are left open, without appropriation to counties—whilst at every other Cambridge College, except King's, territorial restrictions existed till this century. And, besides the College Lecturers, maintenance is assigned to three University Readers. These are the Regius Professors of Divinity, Hebrew, and Greek, who are still on Henry VIII.'s foundation. Thus, from its origin, Trinity College was specially associated with two ideas: free competition of merit; and provision, not only for collegiate tuition, but also for properly academic teaching.

During the first century of its life—from the reign of Edward VI. to the Civil Wars—the prosperity of Trinity College was brilliant and unbroken. The early days of the Great Rebellion were more disastrous for Cambridge than for Oxford; yet at Cambridge, as at Oxford, the period of the Commonwealth was one in which learning throve. Trinity College was "purged" of its Royalist members in 1645. Dr. Thomas Hill then became Master. He proved an excellent administrator. Isaac Barrow, who was an undergraduate of the College, had written an exercise on "the Gunpowder Treason," in which his Cavalier sympathies were frankly avowed. Some of the Fellows were so much incensed that they moved for his expulsion, when Hill silenced them with the words, "Barrow is a better man than any of us." The last Master of Trinity before the Restoration was Dr. John Wilkins, brother-in-law of Oliver Cromwell, and formerly Warden of Wadham College, Oxford; who was "always zealous to promote worthy men and generous designs." He was shrewdly

suspected of being a Royalist, and Cromwell had been wont
to greet his visits thus: "What, brother Wilkins, I suppose you are come to ask something or other in favour of
the Malignants?"   But his influence is said to have decided
the Protector against confiscating the revenues of Oxford
and Cambridge to pay his army.*

In the space of forty years between the Restoration and
Bentley's arrival, Trinity College had suffered some de-
cline; not through any default of eminent abilities or
worthy characters, but partly from general influences of
the time, partly from the occasional want of a sufficiently
firm rule.   Dr. John Pearson—the author of the treatise
on the Creed—was Master of Trinity from 1662 to 1673.
A contemporary—whose words plainly show the contrast
with Bentley which was in his mind—said that Pearson
was "a man the least apt to encroach upon anything that
belonged to the Fellows, but treated them all with abun-
dance of civility and condescension."   "The Fellows, he
has heard, ask'd him whether he wanted anything in his
lodge—table-linen, or the like; 'No,' saith the good man,
'I think not; this I have will serve yet;' and though
pressed by his wife to have new, especially as it was offered him, he would refuse it while the old was fit for use.
He was very well contented with what the College allowed
him."

* See a letter, preserved in the Muniment-room of Trinity College,
Cambridge, and published by Mr. W. Aldis Wright in *Notes and
Queries*, Aug. 13, 1881.   I may remark that Dr. Creyghton, whose
recollections in old age the letter reports, errs in one detail.   It must
have been as Warden of Wadham, not as Master of Trinity, that Wilkins interceded against the confiscation.   Oliver Cromwell died Sept.
3, 1658.   It was early in 1659 that Richard Cromwell appointed
Wilkins to Trinity College.

Pearson was succeeded in the Mastership by Isaac Barrow, who held it for only four years—from 1673 to his death in 1677. Both as a mathematician and as a theologian he stood in the foremost rank. In 1660 he was elected "without a competitor" to the professorship of Greek. Thus a singular triad of distinctions is united in his person; as Lucasian professor of Mathematics, he was the predecessor of Newton; at Trinity College, of Bentley; and, in his other chair, of Porson. In early boyhood he was chiefly remarkable for his pugnacity, and for his aversion to books. When he was at Charterhouse, "his greatest recreation was in such sports as brought on fighting among the boys; in his after-time a very great courage remained . . . yet he had perfectly subdued all inclination to quarrelling; but a negligence of his cloaths did always continue with him." As Master of Trinity, "besides the particular assistance he gave to many in their studies, he concerned himself in everything that was for the interest of his College."

The next two Masters were men of a different type. John North was the fifth son of Dudley, Lord North, and younger brother of Francis North, first Baron Guilford, Lord Keeper in the reigns of Charles II. and James II. He had been a Fellow of Jesus College, and in 1677 he was appointed Master of Trinity. John North was a man of cultivated tastes and considerable accomplishments, of a gentle, very sensitive disposition, and of a highly nervous temperament. Even after he was a Fellow of his College, he once mistook a moonlit towel for "an enorm spectre;" and his brother remembers how, at a still later period, "one Mr. Wagstaff, a little gentleman, had an express audience, at a very good dinner, on the subject of spectres, and much was said *pro* and *con*." On one occasion he travelled into Wales, "to visit and be possessed of his sinecure of Llandinon." "The parishioners came about him and hugged him, calling him their pastor, and telling him they were his sheep;" when "he got him back to his College as fast as he could." In the Mastership of Trinity North showed no weakness. Certain abuses had begun to infect the election to Fellowships, and he made a vigorous effort to remedy them. He was no less firm in his endeavours to revive discipline, which had been somewhat relaxed since the Restoration. One day he was in the act of admonishing two students, when he fell down in a fit. The two young men were "very helpful" in carrying him to the Lodge. Paralysis of one side ensued. He lived for upwards of three years, but could thenceforth take little part in College affairs; and died, six years after he had become Master, in 1683.

Dr. John Mountague, North's successor, was the fourth son of Edward, first Earl of Sandwich. The little that is known of Mountague exhibits him as an amiable person of courtly manners, who passed decently along the path of rapid preferment which then awaited a young divine with powerful connexions. Having first been Master of Sherburn Hospital at Durham, he was appointed, in 1683, to the Mastership of Trinity. His easy temper and kindly disposition made him popular with the Fellows—all the more so, perhaps, if his conscience was less exacting than that of the highly-strung, anxious North. In 1699 he returned, as Dean of Durham, to the scene of his earlier duties, and lived to see the fortunes of the College under Bentley. He died in London, in 1728. There was a double disadvantage for Bentley in coming after such a man; the personal contrast was marked; and those tendencies which North strove to repress had not suffered,

5*

under Mountague, from any interference which exceeded
the limits of good breeding.

In the fore-front of the difficulties which met Bentley
Dr. Monk puts the fact that he "had no previous connexion with the College which he was sent to govern;
he was himself educated in another and a rival society."
Now, without questioning that there were murmurs on
this score, I think that we shall overrate the influence
of such a consideration if we fail to observe what the
precedents had been up to that date. Bentley was the
twentieth Master since 1546. Of his nineteen predecessors, only five had been educated at Trinity College.
To take the four immediately preceding cases, Barrow
and Mountague had been of Trinity, but Pearson had
been of King's, and North of Jesus. Since Bentley's
time every Master has been of Trinity. But it cannot
be said that any established usage then existed of which
Bentley's appointment was a breach. And young though
he was for such a post—thirty-eight—he was not young
beyond recent example. Pearson, when appointed, had
been forty; Barrow, forty-three; North, thirty-three; and
Mountague, only twenty-eight. Thus the choice was not
decidedly exceptional in either of the two points which
might make it appear so now. But the task which, at
that moment, awaited a Master of Trinity was one which
demanded a rare union of qualities. How would Bentley
succeed? A few readers of the Dissertation on Phalaris,
that mock despot of Agrigentum, might tremble a little,
perhaps, at the thought that the scholarly author appeared
to have a robust sense of what a real tyrant should be, and a
cordial contempt for all shams in the part. It was natural,
however, to look with hope to his mental grasp and vigour,
his energy, his penetration, his genuine love of learning.

CHAPTER VII.

When Bentley entered on his new office, he was in one of those positions where a great deal may depend on the impression made at starting. He did not begin very happily. One of his first acts was to demand part of a College dividend due by usage to his predecessor, Dr. Mountague, who closed the discussion by waiving his claim. Then the Master's Lodge required repairs, and the Seniority (the eight Senior Fellows) had voted a sum for that purpose, but the works were executed in a manner which ultimately cost about four times the amount. It is easy to imagine the comments and comparisons to which such things would give rise in a society not, perhaps, too favourably prepossessed towards their new chief. But Bentley's first year at Trinity is marked by at least one event altogether fortunate — his marriage. At Bishop Stillingfleet's house he had met Miss Joanna Bernard, daughter of Sir John Bernard, of Brampton, Huntingdonshire. "Being now raised to a station of dignity and consequence, he succeeded in obtaining the object of his affections," says Dr. Monk—who refuses to believe a story that the engagement was nearly broken off owing to a doubt expressed by Bentley with regard to the authority of the Book of Daniel. Whiston has

told us what this alleged doubt was. Nebuchadnezzar's
golden image is described as sixty cubits high and six
cubits broad; now, said Bentley, this is out of all proportion; it ought to have been ten cubits broad at least;
"which made the good lady weep." The lovers' difference was possibly arranged on the basis suggested by
Whiston — that the sixty cubits included the pedestal.
Some letters which passed between Dr. Bentley and Miss
Bernard, before their marriage, are still extant, and have
been printed by Dr. Luard at the end of Rud's *Diary*.
In the Library of Trinity College is preserved a small
printed and interleaved "Ephemeris" for the year 1701.
The blank page opposite the month of January has the
following entries in Bentley's hand:

"Jan. 4. I maried Mrs. Johanna Bernard, daughter of Sʳ John
Bernard, Baronet. Dʳ Richardson, Fellow of Eaton College and Master of Peterhouse, maried us at Windsor in yᵉ College Chapel.

"6.   I brought my wife to Sᵗ James's [*i. e.*, to his lodgings, as
King's Librarian, in the Palace].

"27. I am 39 years old, complete.

"28. I returnd to ye College."

It was a thoroughly happy marriage, through forty years
of union. What years they were, too, outside of the home
in which Mrs. Bentley's gentle presence dwelt! In days
when evil tongues were busy no word is said of her but
in praise; and perhaps, if all were known, few women ever
went through more in trying, like Mrs. Thrale, to be civil
for two.

Bentley was Vice-chancellor of Cambridge at the time
of his marriage. His year of office brought him into col-
lision with the gaieties of that great East England carni-
val, Sturbridge Fair. Its entertainments were under the
joint control of the University and the Town, but, without

licence from the Vice-chancellor, some actors had been announced to play in September, 1701. Bentley interposed his veto, and provided for discipline by investing sixty-two Masters of Arts with the powers of Proctors. One of his last acts as Vice-chancellor was to draw up an address which the University presented to King William, expressing "detestation of the indignity" which Louis XIV. had just offered to the English Crown by recognising the claims of the Pretender.

The term of his University magistracy having expired, Bentley was able to bestow undivided attention on Trinity College. An important reform was amongst his earliest measures. Fellowships and Scholarships were at that time awarded by a merely oral examination. Written papers were now introduced; the competition for Scholarships became annual instead of biennial, and freshmen were admitted to it. The permanent value of this change is not affected by the estimate which may be formed of Bentley's personal conduct in College elections. There are instances in which it was represented as arbitrary and unfair. But we must remember that his behaviour was closely watched by numerous enemies, who eagerly pressed every point which could be plausibly urged against him. The few detailed accounts which we have of the elections give the impression that, in those cases at least, the merits of candidates were fairly considered. Thus John Byrom says (1709): "We were examined by the Master, Vicemaster, and Dr. Smith, one of the Seniors. On Wednesday we made theme for Dr. Bentley, and on Thursday the Master and Seniors met in the Chapel for the election [to Scholarships]. Dr. Smith had the gout and was not there. They stayed consulting about an hour and a half, and then the Master wrote the names of the elect and gave them to

the Chapel Clerk." Whether he was or was not always
blameless on such occasions, Bentley deserves to be remembered as the Master who instituted a better machin-
ery for testing merit, and provided better guarantees for
its recognition.

To do him justice, no man could have been more earnest than Bentley was in desiring to maintain the prestige
of Trinity College, or more fully sensible of the rank due
to it in science and letters. It was through Bentley's influence that the newly-founded Plumian Professorship of
Astronomy was conferred on Roger Cotes—then only a
Bachelor of Arts—who was provided with an observato-
ry in the rooms over the Great Gate of Trinity College
(1706). Ten years later, when this man of wonderful
promise died at the age of thirty-four, Newton said, " Had
Cotes lived, we should have known something." The appointment of Cotes may be regarded as marking the formal establishment of a Newtonian school in Cambridge;
and it was of happy omen that it should have been first
lodged within the walls which had sheltered the labours
of the founder. Three English sovereigns visited the College in the course of Bentley's Mastership, but the most
interesting fact connected with any of these occasions is
the public recognition of Newton's scientific eminence in
1705, when he received knighthood from Queen Anne at
Trinity Lodge. Then it was Bentley who fitted up a
chemical laboratory in Trinity College for Vigani, a native of Verona, who, after lecturing in Cambridge for some
years, was appointed Professor of Chemistry in 1702. It
was Bentley who made Trinity College the home of the
eminent Oriental scholar Sike, of Bremen, whom he helped
to obtain the Regius Chair of Hebrew in 1703. Briefly,
wherever real science needed protection or encouragement,

there, in Bentley's view, was the opportunity of Trinity College; it was to be indeed a house of the sciences and "of all kinds of good letters;" it was to be not only a great College, but, in its own measure, a true University.

This noble conception represents the good side of Bentley's Mastership; he did something towards making it a reality; he did more still towards creating, or reanimating, a tradition that this is what Trinity College was meant to be, and that nothing lower than this is the character at which it should aim. Nor is it without significance that Nevile's care for the external embellishment of the College was resumed by Bentley. The Chapel, begun in 1557 and finished in Elizabeth's reign, was through Bentley's efforts entirely refitted, and furnished with a fine organ by Bernard Smith. This work was completed in 1727. The grounds beyond the river, acquired by Nevile, were first laid out by Bentley; and the noble avenue of limes, planted in 1674 on the west side of the Cam, was continued in 1717 from the bridge to the College.

But unfortunately it was his resolve to be absolute, and he proclaimed it in a manner which was altogether his own. The College Bursar (a Fellow) having protested against the lavish outlay on the repairs of the Master's Lodge, Bentley said that he would "send him into the country to feed his turkeys." When the Fellows opposed him in the same matter, he alluded to his power, under the Statutes, of forbidding them to leave the College, and cried, "Have you forgotten my rusty sword?" The Fellow who held the office of Junior Bursar had demurred to paying for a hen-house which had been put in the Master's yard; Bentley, doubtless in allusion to Lafontaine's fable of "the Old Lion," replied, "I will not be kicked by

an *ass* "—and presently strained his prerogative by stop-
ping the Junior Bursar's commons. Remonstrances being
made, he grimly rejoined, "'Tis all but *lusus jocusque*
(mere child's-play); I am not warm yet." Criticising a
financial arrangement which was perfectly legitimate, but
of which he disapproved, he accused the Seniors of "rob-
bing the Library," and "putting the money in their own
pockets." He harassed the society by a number of petty
regulations, in which we may give him credit for having
aimed at a tonic effect, but which were so timed and executed as to be highly vexatious. Thus, in order to force
the Fellows to take the higher degrees, he procured the
decision, after a struggle, that any Bachelor or Doctor of
Divinity should have a right to College rooms or a College living before a Master of Arts, even though the latter
was senior on the list of Fellows. As a measure of re-
trenchment, he abolished the entertainment of guests by
the College at the great festivals. Taking the dead letter
of the Statutes in its rigour, he decreed that the College
Lecturers should be fined if they omitted to perform certain daily exercises in the hall, which were no longer need-
ful or valuable; he also enforced, in regard to the thirty
junior Fellows, petty fines for absence from chapel (which
were continued to recent times). On several occasions he
took into his own hands a jurisdiction which belonged to
him only jointly with the eight Seniors. Thus, in one instance, he expelled two Fellows of the College by his sole
fiat.

If Bentley is to be credited with the excellence of the
intentions which declared themselves in such a form, recognition is certainly due to the forbearance shown by the
Fellows of Trinity. Bentley afterwards sought to represent them as worthless men who resented his endeavours

to reform them.   It cannot be too distinctly said that this
was totally unjust.   The Fellows, as a body, were liable
to no such charges as Bentley in his anger brought against
them ; not a few of them were eminent in the University ;
and if there were any whose lives would not bear scrutiny,
they were at most two or three, usually non-resident, and
always without influence.   It may safely be said that no
large society of that time, in either University, would
have sustained an inspection with more satisfactory results.   The average College Fellow of that period was a
moderately accomplished clergyman, whose desire was to
repose in decent comfort on a small freehold.   Bentley
swooped on a large house of such persons—not ideal students, yet, on the whole, decidedly favourable specimens
of their kind ; he made their lives a burden to them, and
then denounced them as the refuse of humanity when
they dared to lift their heads against his insolent assumption of absolute power.   They bore it as long as flesh and
blood could.   For nearly eight years they endured.   At
last, in December, 1709, things came to a crisis—almost
by an accident.

Bentley had brought forward a proposal for redistribut-
ing the divisible income of the College according to a
scheme of his own, one feature of which was that the
Master should receive a dividend considerably in excess of
his legitimate claims.   Even Bentley's authority failed to
obtain the acquiescence of the Seniors in this novel inter-
pretation of the maxim, *divide et impera*.   They declined
to sanction the scheme.   While the discussion was pend-
ing, Edmund Miller, a lay Fellow, came up to spend the
Christmas vacation at Trinity.   As an able barrister, who
understood College business, he was just such an ally as
the Fellows needed.   He found them, he says, "looking

like so many prisoners, which were uncertain whether to
expect military execution, or the favour of decimation."
At a meeting of the Master and Seniors, it was agreed to
hear Miller, as a representative of the junior Fellows, on
the dividend question. Miller denounced the plan to
Bentley's face, who replied by threatening to deprive him
of his Fellowship. A few days later, an open rupture
took place between the Seniors and Bentley, who left the
room exclaiming, "Henceforward, farewell peace to Trinity College." Miller now drew up a declaration, which
was signed by twenty-four resident Fellows, including the
Seniors. It expressed a desire that Bentley's conduct
should be represented "to those who are the proper
judges thereof, and in such manner as counsel shall ad-
vise." Bentley, against the unanimous vote of the Seniors, and on a technical quibble of his own, now declared
Miller's Fellowship void. Miller appealed to the Vice-
master, who, supported by all the Seniors, replaced him
on the list. The Master again struck out his name. Miller now left for London. Bentley soon followed. Both
sides were resolved on war.

Who were "the proper judges" of Bentley's conduct?
The 46th chapter of Edward VI.'s Statutes for Trinity
College recognised the Bishop of Ely as General Visitor.
The Elizabethan Statutes omit this, but in their 40th chapter, which provides for the removal of the Master in case
of necessity, incidentally speak of the Bishop as Visitor.
Bentley, six years before (1703), had himself appealed to
the Bishop of Ely on a point touching the Master's prerogative. No other precedent existed. Acting on this,
the Fellows, in February, 1710, laid their "humble petition and complaint" before the Bishop of Ely. They
brought, in general terms, a charge of malversation against

Bentley, and promised to submit "the several particulars" within a convenient time. Bentley now published a "Letter to the Bishop of Ely," in which he made a most gross attack on the collective character of the Fellows, describing their Petition as "the last struggle and effort of vice and idleness against vertue, learning, and good discipline." In July the Fellows presented "the several particulars" to the Bishop, in the form of an accusation comprising fifty-four counts. The Statute prescribed that an accused Master should be "examined" before the Visitor. Hence each of the counts is interrogative. For example:

"**Why** have you for many Years last past, wasted the College Bread, Ale, Beer, Coals, Wood, Turfe, Sedge, Charcoal, Linnen, Pewter, Corn, Flower, Brawn, and Bran? &c."

"**When** by false and base Practices, as by threatning to bring Letters from Court, Visitations, and the like; and at other times, by boasting of your great Interest and Acquaintance, and that you were the Genius of the Age, and what great things you would do for the College in general, and for every Member of it in particular, and promising that you would for the future live peaceably with them, and never make any farther Demands, you had prevailed with the Senior Fellows to allow you several hundred Pounds for your Lodge, more than they first intended or agreed for, to the great Dissatisfaction of the College, and the wonder of the whole University, and all that heard of it: **Why** did you the very next Year, about that time, merely for your own Vanity, require them to build you a new Staircase in your Lodge? **And when** they (considering how much you had extorted from them before, which you had never accounted for) did for good reason deny to do it: **Why** did you of your own Head pull down a good Stair-case in your Lodge, and give Orders and Directions for building a new one, and that too fine for common Use?"

"**Why** did you use scurrilous Words and Language to several of the Fellows, particularly by calling Mr. *Eden* an Ass, and Mr. *Rashly* the College Dog, and by telling Mr. *Cock* he would die in his Shoes?"

Dr. Moore, the learned Bishop of Ely, was one of the six Commissioners who had nominated Bentley for the Mastership; he sympathised with his studies; and Bentley had been Archdeacon of the diocese since 1701. The judge, then, could hardly be suspected of any bias against the accused. He sent a copy of the accusation to Bentley, who ignored it for some months. In November the Bishop wrote again, requiring a reply by December 18. Bentley then petitioned the Queen, praying that the Bishop of Ely might be restrained from usurping the functions of Visitor. The Visitor of Trinity College, Bentley contended, was the Sovereign. Mr. Secretary St. John at once referred Bentley's contention to the Law Officers of the Crown, and meanwhile the Bishop was inhibited from proceeding. This was at the end of 1710.

Bentley's move was part of a calculation. In 1710 the Tories had come in under Harley and St. John. Mrs. Bentley was related to St. John, and also to Mr. Masham, whose wife had succeeded the Duchess of Marlborough in the Queen's favour. Bentley reckoned on commanding sufficient influence to override the Bishop's jurisdiction by a direct interposition of the Crown. He was disappointed. The Attorney-general and the Solicitor-general reported that, in their opinion, the Bishop of Ely was Visitor of Trinity College in matters concerning the Master; adding that Bentley could, if he pleased, try the question in a court of law. This was not what Bentley desired. He now wrote to the Prime-minister, Harley, who had recently escaped assassination, and, with the office of Lord High Treasurer, had been created Earl of Oxford. Bentley's letter is dated July 12, 1711. " I desire nothing more," he writes, " than that her Majesty would send down commissioners to examine into all matters upon the place,

... and to punish where the faults shall be found. ... I am easy under everything but loss of time by detainment here in town, which hinders me from putting my last hand to my edition of Horace, and from doing myself the honour to inscribe it to your Lordship's great name." The Premier did his best. He referred the report of the Attorney and Solicitor to the Lord Keeper, Sir Simon Harcourt, and Queen's Counsel. In January, 1712, they expressed their opinion that the Sovereign is the General Visitor of Trinity College, but that the Bishop of Ely is Special Visitor in the case of charges brought against the Master. The Minister now tried persuasion with the Fellows. Could they not concur with the Master in referring their grievances to the Crown? The Fellows declined. A year passed. Bentley tried to starve out the College by refusing to issue a dividend. In vain. The Ministry were threatened with a revlsiun, in the Queen's Bench, of their veto on the Bishop. They did not like this prospect. On April 18, 1713, Bolingbroke, as Secretary of State, authorised the Bishop of Ely to proceed.

Bentley's ingenuity was not yet exhausted. He proposed that the trial should be held forthwith at Cambridge, where all the College books were ready to hand. Had this been done, he must certainly have been acquitted, since the prosecutors had not yet worked up their case. Some of the Fellows unwarily consented. But the Bishop appointed Ely House, in London, as the place of trial, and the month of November, 1713, as the time. Various causes of delay intervened. At last, in May, 1714, the trial came on in the great hall of Ely House. Five counsel, including Miller, were employed for the Fellows, and three for Bentley. Bishop Moore had two eminent lawyers as his assessors — Lord Cowper, an ex-

Chancellor, and Dr. Newton. Public feeling was at first with Bentley, as a distinguished scholar and divine. But the prosecutors had a strong case. An anecdote of the trial is given by Bentley's grandson, Cumberland. One day the Bishop intimated, from his place as Judge, that he condemned the Master's conduct. For once, Bentley's iron nerve failed him. He fainted in court.

After lasting six weeks, the trial ended about the middle of June. Both sides now awaited with intense anxiety the judgment of the Bishop and his assessors. The prosecutors were confident. But week after week elapsed in silence. The Bishop had caught a chill during the sittings. On July 31 he died. The next day, August 1, 1714, London was thrilled by momentous news. Queen Anne was no more. The British Crown had passed to the House of Hanover. Ministers had fallen; new men were coming to power; the political world was wild with excitement; and the griefs of Trinity College would have to wait.

Bentley's escape had been narrow. After Bishop Moore's death, the judgment which he had prepared, but not pronounced, was found among his papers: "By this our definitive sentence, we remove Richard Bentley from his office of Master of the College." Dr. Monk thinks that the Bishop had meant this merely to frighten Bentley into a compromise with the Fellows. Possibly; though in that case the Bishop would have had to reckon with the other side. But in any case Bentley must have accepted the Bishop's terms, and these must have been such as would have satisfied the prosecutors. If not ejected, therefore, he would still have been defeated. As it was, he got off scot-free.

The new Bishop of Ely, Dr. Fleetwood, took a different line from his predecessor. The Crown lawyers had held that the Bishop was Special Visitor, but not General Visitor. Dr. Fleetwood said that, if he interfered at all, it must be as General Visitor, to do justice on all alike. This scared some of the weaker Fellows into making peace with Bentley, who kindly consented to drop his dividend scheme. In one sense the new Bishop's course was greatly to Bentley's advantage, since it raised the preliminary question over again. Miller vainly tried to move Dr. Fleetwood. Meanwhile Bentley was acting as autocrat of the College — dealing with its property and its patronage as he pleased. His conduct led to a fresh effort for redress.

The lead on this occasion was taken by Dr. Colbatch, now a Senior Fellow. From the beginning of the feuds, Colbatch had been a counsellor of moderation, disapproving much in the stronger measures advocated by Miller. He was an able and accomplished man, whose rigid maintenance of his own principles extorted respect even where it did not command sympathy. Colbatch's early manhood had been expended on performing the duties of private tutor in two families of distinction, and he had returned to College at forty, more convinced than ever that it is a mistake to put trust in princes. He was a dangerous enemy because he seemed incapable of revenge; it was always on high grounds that he desired the confusion of the wicked; and he pursued that object with the temperate implacability which belongs to a disappointed man of the world. Since the Bishop of Ely would not act unless as General Visitor, Colbatch drew up a petition, which nineteen Fellows signed, praying that it might be ascertained who was General Visitor. This was encouraged by the Archbishop of Canterbury, Dr. Wake—who described Bentley as "the greatest instance of human frailty that I know of, as with such good parts and so much learning he can be so insupportable." The object of the petition was baulked for the time by the delays of the Attorney-general. After three years the petition came before the Privy Council in May, 1719.

Bentley was equal to the occasion. Serjeant Miller had presented the petition, and could withdraw it. For five years Bentley had been making active war on Miller, and renewing the attempt to eject him from his Fellowship. Now, towards the end of 1719, he made peace with him, on singular terms. Miller was to withdraw the petition; to resign his Fellowship, in consideration of certain payments; and to receive the sum of £400 as costs on account of the former prosecution before Bishop Moore. Miller agreed. Bentley then proposed the compact to the Seniors. Five of the eight would have nothing to say to it. By a series of manœuvres, however, Bentley carried it at a subsequent meeting. Serjeant Miller received £528 from the College. Who shall describe the feelings of the belligerent Fellows, when the Serjeant's strategy collapsed in this miserable Sedan? It was he who had made them go to war; it was he who had led them through the mazes of the law; they had caught his clear accents, learned his great language; and here was the end of it! But this was not all. If the College is to pay costs on one side, the Master argued, it must pay them on both. Accordingly, Bentley himself received £500 for his own costs in the trial. And, anxious to make hay in this gleam of sunshine, he further prevailed on the Seniors to grant a handsome sum for certain furniture of the Master's Lodge. Bentley had no more to fear, at present, from the opposition of an organised party. For the next few years his encounters were single combats.

Such was the state of affairs in Trinity College. Meanwhile Bentley's relations with the University had come to an extraordinary pass. From the first days of his Mastership his reputation, his ability and energy had made him influential in Cambridge, though he was not generally popular. We saw that, before his appointment to Trinity, he had taken a leading part in the reparation of the University Press. He continued to show an active interest in its management by serving on occasional committees; no permanent Press Syndicate was constituted till 1737. Politics were keen at the University in Bentley's time: a division in the academic Senate was often a direct trial of strength between Whig and Tory. When Bentley struck a blow in these University battles, it was almost always with a view to some advantage in his own College war. Two instances will illustrate this. In June, 1712, when acting as Deputy Vice-chancellor, Bentley carried in the Senate an address to Queen Anne, congratulating her on the progress of the peace negotiations at Utrecht. The address was meant as a manifesto in support of the Tory Ministry, whom the Whigs had just been attacking on this score in the Lords. At that time Harley, the Tory Premier, was the protector on whom Bentley relied in his College troubles. The irritation of the Whig party in the University may have been one cause of a severe reflection passed on Bentley soon afterwards. The Senate resolved that no Archdeacon of Ely should thenceforth be eligible as Vice-chancellor; a decree which, however, was rescinded two years later. Then in 1716 Bentley sorely needed the countenance of the Whig Government against the revived hostilities in Trinity. By a surprise he carried through the Senate an address to George I., congratulating him on the recent suppression of the Jacobite risings.

6

A letter of Bentley's describes the Cambridge Tories as being "in a desperate rage"—not wholly, perhaps, without provocation.

It was shortly before this—in the early days of the Jacobite rebellion, when visions of a Roman Catholic reign were agitating the public imagination—that Bentley preached before the University, on the 5th of November, 1715, his "Sermon on Popery"—from which a passage on the tortures of the Inquisition has been transferred by Sterne to the pages of "Tristram Shandy," and deeply moves Corporal Trim. Bentley had then lately received the unusual honour of being publicly thanked by the Senate for his reply to "A Discourse of Free-thinking" by Anthony Collins. When the Regius Professorship of Divinity—the most valuable in the University—fell vacant in 1717, few persons, perhaps, would have questioned Dr. Bentley's claims on the grounds of ability and learning. But the Statute had declared that the Professor must not hold any other office in the University or in Trinity College. Two precedents were alleged to show that a Master of Trinity might hold the Professorship, but they were not unexceptionable. Of the seven electors, three certainly—presumably five—were against the Master of Trinity's pretensions. The favourite candidate was Dr. Ashton, Master of Jesus; and there are letters to him which show the strong feeling in the University against his rival. On the whole, most men would have despaired. Not so Bentley. By raising a legal point, he contrived to stave off the election for a few weeks; and then seized a propitious moment. The Vice-chancellor was one of the seven electors. It was arranged that Mr. Grigg, who held that office, should leave Cambridge for a few days, naming Bentley Deputy Vice-chancellor. On the day of election the Master of Trinity was chosen Regius Professor of Divinity by four out of seven votes, one of the four being that of the Deputy Vice-chancellor. It was in this candidature that Dr. Bentley delivered an admired discourse on the three heavenly witnesses, which denied the authenticity of that text. It is no longer extant, but had been seen by Porson, who himself wrote on the subject.

This was in May, 1717. Not long afterwards Bentley had occasion to appear publicly in his new character of Regius Professor. Early in October, George I. was staying at Newmarket. On Friday, the 4th, his Majesty consented to visit Cambridge on the following Sunday. There was not much time for preparation, but it was arranged to confer the degree of Doctor of Laws on twenty-seven of the royal retinue, and that of Doctor of Divinity on thirty-two members of the University. On Sunday morning Mr. Grigg, the Vice-chancellor, presented himself at Trinity Lodge, there to await the arrival of the Chancellor, "the proud Duke of Somerset." Bentley was unprepared for this honour; he was "in his morning gown," busied with meditations of hospitality or of eloquence; in fact, he remonstrated; but Mr. Grigg remained. At last the Chancellor came. Bentley was affable, but a little *distrait*. "While he entertained the Duke in discourse," says one who was present, "there stood the Earl of Thomond and Bishop of Norwich, unregarded: and there they might have stood, if one of the Beadles had not touched his sleeve a little; and then he vouchsafed them a welcome also." But worse was to come. George I. attended service at King's College Chapel. When it was over, the Vice-chancellor proceeded to conduct his Majesty back to Trinity College. But Mr. Grigg was desirous that royal eyes should behold his own College, Clare Hall, and there-

fore chose a route which led to a closed gate of Trinity
College. Here a halt of some minutes took place in a
muddy lane, before word could reach the principal en-
trance, where Bentley and an enthusiastic crowd were
awaiting their Sovereign.

These little griefs, however, were nothing to the later
troubles which this day's proceedings begat for Bentley.
As it was thought that thirty-two new Doctors of Divinity
might be too much for the King, Sunday's ceremonial had
been limited to presenting a few of them as samples.
Bentley, as Regius Professor of Divinity, had done his
part admirably. But the next day, when the rest of the
doctors were to be " created " at leisure, Bentley flatly refused to proceed, unless each of them paid him a fee of
four guineas, in addition to the customary broad-piece.
As the degrees were honorary, the claim was sheer extortion. Some complied, others resisted. Conyers Middleton, the biographer of Cicero, was at this time a resident
in Cambridge, though no longer a Fellow of any College.
He paid his four guineas, got his D.D. degree, and then
sued Bentley for the debt in the Vice-chancellor's Court,
a tribunal of academic jurisdiction in such matters. After
months of fruitless diplomacy, the Vice-chancellor reluc-
tantly issued a decree for Bentley's arrest at Middleton's
suit. The writ was served on Bentley at Trinity Lodge—
not, however, before one of the Esquire Bedells had been
treated with indignity. Bail was given for Bentley's appearance before the Court on October 3, 1718. He failed
to appear. The Court then declared that he was suspended from all his degrees. A fortnight later, a Grace was
offered to the Senate, proposing that Bentley's degrees
should be not merely suspended but taken away. Bentley's friends did their utmost. To the honour of the Fel-

lows of Trinity, only four of them voted against him.
But the Grace was carried by more than two to one.
Nine Heads of Colleges and twenty-three Doctors sup-
ported it.

When the Master of Trinity learned that he was no
longer Richard Bentley, D.D., M.A., or even B.A., but
simply Richard Bentley, he said, "I have rubbed through
many a worse business than this." He instantly bestirred
himself with his old vigour, petitioning the Crown, appealing to powerful friends, and dealing some hard knocks in
the free fight of pamphlets which broke out on the question. For nearly six years, however, he remained under
the sentence of degradation. During that period he
brought actions of libel against his two principal adversaries, Colbatch, and Conyers Middleton. Colbatch suffered
a week's imprisonment and a fine. Middleton was twice
prosecuted; the first time, he had to apologise to Bentley,
and pay costs; the second time he was fined. During the
years 1720–1723 Bentley had altogether six lawsuits in
the Court of King's Bench, and gained all of them. The
last and most important was against the University, for
having taken away his degrees. That act had undoubtedly
been illegal. The four Judges all took Bentley's part.
On February 7, 1724, the Court gave judgment. The
University received peremptory direction to restore Bentley's degrees. That command was obeyed, but with a
significant circumstance. On March 25, 1724, the Vice-
chancellor was to lay the first stone of the new buildings
designed for King's College. In order that Bentley might
not participate as a Doctor in the ceremonial, the Grace restoring his degrees was offered to the Senate on March 26.

Thus, after fifteen years of almost incessant strife, the
Master of Trinity had prevailed over opposition both in

the College and in the University. He was sixty-two.
His fame as a scholar was unrivalled. As a controversialist he had proved himself a match, in different fields, for
wits, heretics, and lawyers. At Cambridge, where he was
now the virtual leader of the Whig party in the Senate,
his influence had become pre-eminent. And as if to show
that he had passed through all his troubles without stain,
it was in this year, 1724, that the Duke of Newcastle
wrote and offered him the Bishopric of Bristol — then
rather a poor one. Bentley declined it, frankly observing
that the revenues of the see would scarcely enable him to
attend Parliament. When he was asked what preferment
he would accept — "Such," he answered, "as would not
induce me to desire an exchange."

The remainder of this combative life, it might have been
thought, would now be peaceful. But the last chapter is
the most curious of all. It can be briefly told. Dr. Colbatch, the ablest of Bentley's adversaries in Trinity College, had never resigned the purpose of bringing the Master to justice. It had become the object for which he
lived : private wrongs had sunk into his mind; but he
believed himself to be fulfilling a public duty. In 1726
he vainly endeavoured to procure intervention by the Dean
and Chapter of Westminster, on the ground of certain
grievances suffered by the Westminster scholars at Trinity College. In 1728 he was more successful. Some Fellows of Trinity joined him in a fresh attempt to obtain
a visitation of the College by the Bishop of Ely. There
was, in fact, good reason for it. Bentley's rule had become practically absolute, and therefore unconstitutional.
While Colbatch's new allies were preparing their measures death nearly saved them the trouble. George II. had
visited Cambridge, and had been received in full state at

Trinity College. Bentley, who was subject to severe colds, had caught a chill during the ceremonies of the reception, in the course of which he had been called on to present no fewer than fifty-eight Doctors of Divinity. He was seized with fever. For some days his life was in most imminent danger. But he rallied, and, after taking the waters at Bath, recovered. Five Counsel having expressed an opinion that the Bishop of Ely was General Visitor of the College, Dr. Greene, who now held that see, cited Bentley to appear before him. Bentley did so; but presently obtained a rule from the Court of King's Bench, staying the Bishop's proceedings on the ground that the articles of accusation included matters not cognizable by the Bishop. The question of the Bishop's jurisdiction was next brought before the King's Bench. The Court decided that the Bishop was in this cause Visitor — but again stayed his proceedings — this time on the ground of a technical informality. The prosecutors now appealed to the House of Lords. The House of Lords reversed the decision of the King's Bench, and empowered the Bishop to try Bentley on twenty of the sixty-four counts which had been preferred.

After the lapse of nearly twenty years, Bentley was once more arraigned at Ely House. This second trial began on June 13, 1733. On April 27, 1734, the Bishop gave judgment. Bentley was found guilty of dilapidating the College goods and violating the College Statutes. He was sentenced to be deprived of the Mastership.

At last the long chase was over and the prey had been run to earth. No shifts or doublings could save him now. It only remained to execute the sentence. The Bishop sent down to Cambridge three copies of his judgment. One was for Bentley. Another was to be posted on the gates of Trinity College. A third was to be placed in the hands of the Vice-master.

The fortieth Statute of Elizabeth, on which the judgment rested, prescribes that the Master, if convicted by the Visitor, shall be deprived *by the agency of the Vicemaster*. It has been thought—and Monk adopts the view —that the word *Vice-master* here is a mere clerical error for *Visitor*. The tenor of the Statute itself first led me to doubt this plausible theory. For it begins by saying that a peccant Master shall first be *admonished* by the Vice-master and Seniors: *per Vice Magistrum*, etc., . . . *admoneatur*. If obdurate, he is then to be examined by the Visitor; and, if convicted, *per eundem Vice-magistrum Officio Magistri privetur*. This seems to mean: "let him be *deprived* by the same Vice-master who had first *admonished* him." The Statute intended to provide for the *execution* of the sentence by the College itself, without the scandal of any external intervention beyond the purely *judicial* interposition of the Visitor. I have since learned that the late Francis Martin, formerly Vice-master, discussed this point in a short paper (Nov. 12, 1857), which Dr. Luard's kindness has enabled me to see. Dr. Monk had seen a copy of the Statutes in which *Visitatorem* was written as a correction over *Vice-magistrum*. He believed this copy to be the original one; and when in 1846 Martin showed him the really authentic copy—with Elizabeth's signature and the Great Seal—in the Muniment-room, he at once said, "I never saw that book." There the words stand clearly *Vice-magrm*, as in the Statutes of Philip and Mary; there is no correction, superscript or marginal; and the vellum shows that there has been no erasure. The Vice-master, who takes the chief part in admitting the Master (Stat. Cap. 2), is the natural minister of depriva-

tion.   Bentley's Counsel advised the Vice-master, Dr.
Hacket, to refrain from acting until he had taken legal
opinion.   Meanwhile Bentley continued to act as Master,
to the indignation of his adversaries, and the astonishment
of the world.   An examination for College scholarships
was going on just then.   On such occasions in former
years Bentley had often set the candidates to write on
some theme suggestive of his own position.   Thus, at the
height of his monarchy, he gave them, from Virgil, " No
one of this number shall go away without a gift from
me;" and once, at a pinch in his wars, from Homer, "De-
spoil others, but keep hands off Hector."   This time he
had a very apposite text for the young composers, from
Terence: " This is your plea now—that I have been turned
out: look you, there are ups and downs in all things."
Dr. Hacket, however, had no mind to stand long in the
breach; and on May 17, 1734, he resigned the Vice-mas-
tership.   He was succeeded by Dr. Richard Walker, a
friend on whom Bentley could rely.   During the next
four years, every resource which ingenuity could suggest
was employed to force Dr. Walker into executing the sentence of deprivation on Bentley.   A petition was presented by Colbatch's party to the House of Lords, which the
peers, after a debate, permitted to be withdrawn.   Dr.
Walker now effected a compromise between Bentley and
some of the hostile Fellows.   But Colbatch persevered.
Three different motions were made in the Court of King's
Bench; first, for a writ to compel Dr. Walker to act;
next, for a writ to compel the Bishop of Ely to compel
Dr. Walker to act; then, for a writ to compel the Bishop
to do his own duty as General Visitor.   All in vain.   On
April 22, 1738, the Court rejected the last of these appli-
cations.

6*

That day marks the end of the strife begun in February, 1710 : it had thus lasted a year longer than the Peloponnesian War. It has two main chapters. The first is the fourteen years' struggle from 1710 to 1724, in which Miller was the leader down to his withdrawal in 1719. The years 1725–1727 were a pause. Then the ten years' struggle, from 1728 to 1738, was organised and maintained by Colbatch. Meanwhile many of the persons concerned were advanced in age. Three weeks after the King's Bench had refused the third mandamus, Bishop Greene died at the age of eighty. Dr. Colbatch was seventy-five. Bentley himself was seventy-seven. If he had wanted another classical theme for the candidates in the scholarship examination, he might have given them —"One man by his delay hath restored our fortunes." He was under sentence of deprivation, but only one person could statutably deprive him ; that person declined to move ; and no one could make him move. Bentley therefore remained master of the field—and of the College.

We remember the incorrigible old gentleman in the play, whose habit of litigation was so strong that, when precluded from further attendance on the public law-courts, he got up a little law-court at home, and prosecuted his dog. Bentley's occupation with the King's Bench ceased in April, 1738. In July he proceeded against Dr. Colbatch at Cambridge in the Consistorial Court of the Bishop of Ely, for the recovery of certain payments called "proxies," alleged to be due from Colbatch, as Rector of Orwell, to Bentley, as Archdeacon of the diocese. The process lasted eighteen months, at the end of which Dr. Colbatch had to pay six years' arrears and costs.

Looking back on Bentley's long war with the Fellows,

one asks, Who was most to blame? De Quincey approves
Dr. Parr's opinion—expressed long after Bentley's death
—that the College was wrong, and Bentley right. But
De Quincey goes further. Even granting that Bentley
was wrong, De Quincey says, we ought to vote him right,
"for by this means the current of one's sympathy with
an illustrious man is cleared of ugly obstructions." It is
good to be in sympathy with an illustrious man, but it is
better still to be just. The merits of the controversy between Bentley and the Fellows have two aspects, legal and
moral. The legal question is simple. Had Bentley, as
Master, brought himself within the meaning of the fortieth Elizabethan Statute, and deserved the penalty of deprivation? Certainly he had. It was so found on two
distinct occasions, twenty years apart, after a prolonged
investigation by lawyers. Morally, the first question is:
Was Bentley obliged to break the Statutes in order to
keep some higher law? He certainly was not. It cannot be shown that the Statutes were in conflict with any
project which he entertained for the good of the College;
and, if they had been so, the proper course for him was
not to violate them, but to move constitutionally for their
alteration. A further moral question concerns the nature
of his personal conduct towards the Fellows. This conduct might conceivably have been so disinterested and
considerate as to give him some equitable claim on their
forbearance, though they might feel bound to resist the
course which he pursued. His conduct was, in fact, of an
opposite character. On a broad view of the whole matter,
from 1710 to 1738, the result is this. Legally, the College had been right, and Bentley wrong. Morally, there
had been faults on both parts; but it was Bentley's intol-
erable behaviour which first, and after long forbearance,

forced the Fellows into an active defence of the common
interests. The words "Farewell peace to Trinity College" were pronounced by Bentley. It is not a relevant
plea that his academic ideal was higher than that of the
men whose rights he attacked.

The College necessarily suffered for a time from these
long years of domestic strife which had become a public
scandal. Almost any other society, perhaps, would have
been permanently injured. But Trinity College had the
strength of unique traditions, deeply rooted in the history
of the country ; and the excellent spirit shown by its best
men, in the time which immediately followed Bentley's,
soon dispelled the cloud. When the grave had closed
over those feuds, the good which Bentley had done lived
in better tests of merit, and in the traditional association
of the College with the encouragement of rising sciences.

Now we must turn to an altogether different side which,
throughout these stormy years, is presented by the activity
of this extraordinary man.

CHAPTER VIII.

FROM the beginning of 1700 to the summer of 1702 Bentley was constantly occupied with University or College affairs. On August 2, 1702, he writes to Graevius at Utrecht: "You must know that for the last two years I have hardly had two days free for literature." This was perhaps the longest decisive interruption of literary work in his whole life. Nearly all his subsequent writings were finished in haste, and many of them were so timed as to appear at moments when he had a special reason for wishing to enlist sympathy. But his studies, as distinguished from his acts of composition, appear to have been seldom broken off for more than short spaces, even when he was most harassed by external troubles. His wonderful nerve and will enabled him to concentrate his spare hours on his own reading, at times when other men would have been able to think of nothing but threatened ruin.

His early years at Trinity College offer several instances of his generous readiness to help and encourage other scholars. One of these was Ludolph Küster, a young Westphalian then living at Cambridge, whom Bentley assisted with an edition of the Greek lexicographer Suidas, and afterwards with an edition of Aristophanes. Another was a young Dutchman, destined to celebrity—Tiberius

Hemsterhuys. Bentley had sent him a kindly criticism on an edition of Julius Pollux, pointing out certain defects of metrical knowledge. The effect on Hemsterhuys has been described by his famous pupil, David Ruhnken. At first he was plunged in despair: then he roused himself to intense effort. To his dying day he revered Bentley, and would hear nothing against him. The story recalls that of F. Jacobs, the editor of the Greek Anthology, who was spurred into closer study of metre by the censures of Godfrey Hermann. In 1709 John Davies, Fellow of Queens' College, Cambridge, published an edition of Cicero's "Tusculan Disputations," with an appendix of critical notes by Bentley. The notes were disparaged in a review called the *Bibliothèque Choisie* by the Swiss John Le Clerc, then leader of the Arminians in Holland; a versatile but shallow man, who had touched the surface of philosophy, and was now ambitious of figuring on the surface of classical literature. Some months later Le Clerc edited the fragments of the Greek comic poets, Menander and Philemon. Nettled by the review, Bentley wrote his own emendations on 323 of these fragments. He restored them metrically, showing that Le Clerc had mixed them with words from the prose texts in which they occur, and had then cut the compound into lengths of twelve syllables, regardless of scansion. Bentley's manuscript, under the name of "Phileleutherus Lipsiensis," was transmitted to a scholar at Utrecht, Peter Burmann, who willingly used the permission to publish it. The first edition was sold in three weeks. Le Clerc learned who "Phileleutherus" was, and wrote a violent letter to Bentley. Bentley made a caustic reply. He has been charged with denying the authorship. He does not do so; but he shows a mischievous pleasure in puzzling his furious correspondent.

As early as 1702 Bentley had been meditating an edition of Horace. I translate from his Latin preface his own account of the motive:

"When, a few years ago [*i. e.*, in 1700], I was promoted to a station in which official duties and harassing cares, daily surging about me, had distracted me from all deeper studies, I resolved—in order that I might not wholly forget the Muses and my old loves—to set about editing some writer of the pleasanter sort, comparatively light in style and matter, such as would make in me, rather than claim from me, a calm and untroubled mind; a work that could be done bit by bit at odd hours, and would brook a thousand interruptions without serious loss. My choice was HORACE; not because I deemed that I could restore and correct more things in him than in almost any other Latin or Greek author; but because he, above all the ancients—thanks to his merit, or to a peculiar genius and gift for pleasing—was familiar to men's hands and hearts. The form and scope of my work I defined and limited thus;—that I should touch only those things which concern the soundness and purity of the *text;* but should wholly pass by the mass of those things which relate to history and ancient manners—that vast domain and laboratory of *comment.*"

Bentley began printing his Horace, with his own emendations embodied in the text and the common readings given at the foot of the page, before he had written the critical notes which were to justify these changes. In August, 1706, he says: "I have printed three new sheets in it this last fortnight, and I hope shall go on to finish by next spring." Sinister auguries were already heard in certain quarters. "I do not wonder," he writes to a friend, "that some . . . do talk so wildly about my Hor-

ace. . . . I am assured none of them will write against my
notes. They have had enough of me, and will hereafter
let me alone." The rumour of Bentley's new labours inspired his old enemy, Dr. King, with a satire called "Horace in Trinity College." Horace is supposed to have fulfilled his dream of visiting our remote island (*visam Bri-
tannos*), but to have lost the airy form in which he proposed to make that excursion—under the influence of
solid cheer supplied to him from the butteries of Trinity
College.

Instead of appearing in the spring of 1707, Bentley's
Horace was not ready till December 8, 1711. The summer months were the only part of the year in which he
could do much; and from his preface it would appear
that between 1702 and 1711 there had been four sum-
mers in which he made no progress. The notes on the
text fill 448 quarto pages of small print, in double column,
at the end of the volume. It is characteristic of Bentley
that a great part of these notes were written in about five
months—July to November, 1711. He says himself that
his work was thrown off "in the first impetus and glow"
of his thoughts, and sent to the press almost before the
ink was dry. It was rather his way to brag of this; but
it must be literally true, to a great extent, of the notes.
He had his own reasons for haste, and worked at high
pressure. The Horace was to be an offering to Harley,
who just then was the umpire of Bentley's fortunes. In
the dedication to the Tory Premier, Bentley openly announces himself as a converted Whig, by saying that
Mæcenas did not like Horace the less for having borne
arms with Brutus and Cassius; not a very happy allusion,
when one remembers that the poet ran away at Philippi.

Bentley's Horace is a monumental proof of his in-

genuity, learning, and argumentative skill. The notes
abound in hints on grammar and metre which have a general value. In reading them one feels, too, the "impetus
and glow " of which their author speaks: one feels almost
everywhere the powerful genius of the man. But while
the Horace shows Bentley's critical method on a large
scale and in a most striking form, it illustrates his defects
as conspicuously as his strength. Bentley had first displayed his skill by restoring deeply corrupted passages of
Greek writers, especially poets. Heroic remedies were
required there. With his wide reading, unrivalled metrical knowledge, and keen insight, Bentley had been able to
make some restorations which seemed little short of mirac-
ulous. Hopeless nonsense, under his touch, became lucid
and coherent. The applause which followed these efforts
exalted his confidence in his own gift of divination. His
mind was confirmed in a bent which kept him constantly
on the lookout for possible improvements of word or
phrase in everything that he read.

Now, Horace was one of the most perilous subjects
that Bentley could have chosen. Not so much because
the text of Horace, as we have it, is particularly pure.
There are many places in which corruption is certain, and
conjecture is the only resource. But, owing to his peculiar cast of mind and style, Horace is one of the very last
authors whose text should be touched without absolute
necessity. In the Satires and Epistles his language is
coloured by two main influences, subtly interfused, each
of which is very difficult, often impossible, for a modern
reader to seize. One is the colloquial idiom of Roman
society. The other is literary association, derived from
sources, old Italian or Greek, which in many cases are
lost. In the Odes, the second of these two influences is

naturally predominant; and in them the danger of tampering is more obvious, though perhaps not really greater, than in the Satires or Epistles. Now, Bentley's tendency was to try Horace by the tests of clear syntax, strict logic, and normal usage. He was bent on making Horace "sound" in a sense less fine, but even more rigorous, than that in which Pope is "correct."

Thus, in the "Art of Poetry," Horace is speaking of a critic: "If you told him, *after two or three vain attempts,* that you could not do better, he would bid you erase your work, and put your *ill-turned verses on the anvil* again" (*et male tornatos incudi reddere versus*). "Ill-turned"— "anvil!" said Bentley: "what has a lathe to do with an anvil?" And so, for *male tornatos,* he writes *male ter natos,* "thrice shaped amiss." Horace elsewhere speaks of verses as *incultis . . . et male natis.* To Bentley's reading, however, it may be objected that the order of words required by the sense is *ter male natos :* for *male ter natos* ought to mean, either "unhappily thrice-born"—like the soul of a Pythagorean, unfortunate in two migrations; or "barely thrice-born"—as if, in some process which required three refinements, the third was scarcely completed. And then, if we are not satisfied with the simplest account of *tornatos*—viz., that Horace lapsed into a mixture of common metaphors—it admits of a strict defence. The verses have been put on the lathe, but have not been successfully rounded and polished. Then, says Horace's critic, they must go back to the *anvil,* and be forged anew, passing again through that first process by which the rough material is brought into shape for the lathe. Yet Bentley was so sure of his *ter natos* that persons who doubted it seemed no better than "moles."

Another instance will illustrate the danger of altering

touches in Horace which may have been suggested by
some lost literary source.   In the Odes (III. iv. 45) Horace
speaks of Jupiter as ruling " *cities* and troubled realms, and
gods, and *the multitudes of men* " (urbes . . . mortalisque
turbas).   " Tell me, pray," cries Bentley, " what is the
sense of ' cities ' and ' the multitudes of men?'   This is
silly—mere tautology."   And so he changes *urbes*, "cities,"
into *umbras*, " the shades " of the departed.   Now, as
Munro has pointed out, Horace may have had in mind a
passage in the *Epicharmus*, a philosophical poem by Ennius, of which a few lines remain : where it is said of Jupiter, " *mortalis atque urbes* beluasque omnes iuvat."   One
or two of Bentley's corrections are not only admirable but
almost certain (as *musto* Falerno for *misto* in the Satires
II. iv. 19).   A few more have reason wholly on their side,
and yet are not intrinsically probable.   Thus in the Epistles
(I. vii. 29) we have the fable of the fox, who, when lean,
crept through a chink into a granary, and there grew too
fat to get out again.   "To the rescue," exclaims Bentley,
" ye sportsmen, rustics, and naturalists!   A fox eating
grain !"   And so Bentley changes the fox into a field-
mouse (*volpecula* into *nitedula*).   But the old fabulist
from whom Horace got the story, meaning to show how
cunning greed may overreach itself, had chosen the animal
which is the type of cunning, without thinking of the
points on which Bentley dwells, the structure of its teeth
and its digestive organs.

Bentley has made altogether between 700 and 800
changes in the text of Horace : in his preface, he recalls
19 of these, but adds a new one (*rectis* oculis for *siccis* in
Odes I. iii. 18 : which convinced Porson).   His paramount
guide, he declares, has been his own faculty of divination.
To this, he says, he has owed more corrections, and cor-

rections of greater certainty, than to the manuscripts—in using which, however, where he does use them, he nearly always shows the greatest tact. Now, criticism of a text has only one proper object—to exhibit what the author wrote. It is a different thing to show what he might have written. Bentley's passion for the exercise of his divining faculty hindered him from keeping this simple fact clearly before his mind. In the "Art of Poetry" (60) Horace has: "*Ut silvae foliis pronos mutantur in annos:*" "As woods suffer change of leaves with each declining year." Nothing could be less open to suspicion—*foliis* being an ordinary ablative of the part affected (like *capti auribus et oculis* for "deaf and blind"). Yet Bentley must needs change this good line into one which is bad both in style and in metre: "*Ut silvis folia privos mutantur in annos,*" "As woods have their leaves changed with each year;" and this he prints in his text. Speaking of Bentley's readings in the mass, one may say that Horace would probably have liked two or three of them—would have allowed a very few more as not much better or worse than his own—and would have rejected the immense majority with a smile or a shudder.

On the other hand, there is a larger sense in which Bentley's Horace is a model of conservative prudence. Recent German criticism has inclined to the view that Horace's works are interpolated not only with spurious passages but with whole spurious poems. Thus Mr. O. F. Gruppe actually rejects the whole of the beautiful ode, *Tyrrhena Regum Progenies* (III. xxix.). Another critic, Mr. Hofmann-Peerlkamp, regrets that Bentley's haste blinded him to many interpolations. Haupt, Meineke, Ritschl have favoured the same tendency. The prevailing view of English scholarship is that the solitary interpolation in our

Horace consists of the eight lines (" *Lucili quam sis men-dosus*," &c.) prefixed to Satire I. 10, and probably as old, or nearly so, as the poem itself. Bentley's suspicions are confined to a few single lines here and there. But there is only one line in all Horace which he positively con-demns. It is mainly a point of literary criticism, and is a curious example of his method. I give it in Latin and English (Odes IV. viii. 15) :

> " Non celeres fugae
>   Reiectaeque retrorsum Hannibalis minae,
>   *Non incendia Carthaginis impiae*
>   Eius qui domita nomen ab Africa
>   Lucratus rediit clarius indicant
>   Laudes, quam Calabrae Pierides."

> " Not the swift flight
>   And menace backward hurled of Hannibal,
>   *Not impious Carthage sinking into fire*
>   So well gives forth his praises, who returned
>   With title won from conquered Africa,
>   As ye, Calabria's Muses."

Now, says Bentley, the Scipio (Africanus maior) who defeated Hannibal in the Second Punic War is a differ-ent person from the Scipio (Africanus minor) who burned Carthage more than half a century later. How can it be said that the defeat of Hannibal glorifies the destroyer of Carthage ? And so Bentley would leave out the burning of Carthage, and make the whole passage refer to the con-queror of Hannibal. The answer seems plain. Horace means : " The glory of the Scipios never reached a higher pinnacle than that on which it was placed by the Cala-brian poet Ennius, when he described the defeat of Han-nibal by the elder Africanus ; though that achievement was crowned by the younger Africanus, when he finally

destroyed Carthage." The "praises" of the younger Africanus are not exclusively his personal exploits, but the
glories, both ancestral and personal, of his name. Then
Bentley objects to the caesura in "*Non incendia Carth|a-
ginis impiae.*" But what of the undoubtedly genuine
verse, "*Dum flagrantia de|torquet ad oscula*" (Odes II.
xii. 25)? "The preposition *de*," he replies, "is, as it
were, separated from the verb *torquet*—not being a native
part of that word." This might seem a bold plea; but
it shows his knowledge. In old Latin inscriptions the
preposition and the rest of the word are often disjoined—
for instance, IN VICTO could stand for INVICTO: and Bentley's principle would apply to Horace's "*Arcanique fides
prodiga per|lucidior vitro*" (Odes I. xviii. 16). If, how-
ever, *Carthaginis* has not the privilege of a compound, it
may have that of a proper name. The presence of a
proper name has been urged in excuse of "*Mentemque
lymphat|am Mareotico*" (Od. I. xxxvii. 14), "*Spectandus
in cert|amine Martio*" (Od. IV. xiv. 17). Bentley does not
notice this ground of defence. Finally, he rejects "Non
incendia Carthaginis impiae" as a verse of "manifestly
monkish spirit and colour."

Bentley was the first modern editor who followed the
best ancient authorities in calling the Odes *Carmina*, and
not *Odae*, the Satires *Sermones*, and not *Satirae*. In his
preface he endeavours to settle the chronological order of
Horace's writings. Previous Horatian critics—as Faber,
Dacier, Masson — had aimed at dating separate poems.
Bentley maintains — rightly, no doubt — that the poems
were originally *published*, as we have them, in whole
books. He further assumes—with much less probability
—that Horace *composed* in only one style at a time, first
writing satires; then iambics (the "Epodes"); then the •

Odes—of which book IV. and the Carmen Saeculare came between the two books of Epistles. Bentley's method is too rigid. He argues from the internal evidence too much as if a poet's works were the successive numbers of a newspaper. Yet here, too—though some of his particular views are arbitrary or wrong—he laid down the main lines of a true scheme.

Bentley's Horace immediately brought out half a dozen squibs—none of them good—and one or two more serious attacks. John Ker, a school-master, assailed Bentley's Latinity in four Letters (1713); and some years later the same ground was taken by Richard Johnson—who had been a contemporary of Bentley's at Cambridge, and was now master of Nottingham School—in his "*Aristarchus Anti-Bentleianus*" (1717). The fact is that Bentley wrote Latin as he wrote English—with racy vigour, and with a wealth of trenchant phrases; but he was not minutely Ciceronian. The two critics were able to pick some holes. One of Bentley's slips was amusing; he promises the readers of his Horace that they will find purity of idiom in his Latin notes—and calls it *sermonis puritatem*—which happens *not* to be pure Latin. In 1721 a rival Horace was published by Alexander Cunningham, a Scottish scholar of great learning and industry. His emendations are sometimes execrable, but often most ingenious. His work is marred, however, by a mean spite against Bentley, whom he constantly tries to represent as a plagiarist or a blunderer—and who ignored him.

The first edition of Bentley's Horace (1711) went off rapidly, and a second was required in 1712. This was published by the eminent firm of Wetstein at Amsterdam. Paper and printing were cheaper there — an important point when the book was to reach all scholars. Thomas

Bentley, the nephew, brought out a smaller edition of the work in 1713, dedicating it—with logical propriety—to Harley's *son*. The line in the *Dunciad* (II. 205)—"Bentley his mouth with classic flatt'ry opes "—is fixed by Warburton on Thomas Bentley, "a small critic, who aped his uncle in a little Horace." Among other compliments, Bentley received one or two which he could scarcely have anticipated. Le Clerc, whom he had just been lashing so unmercifully, wrote a review in the *Bibliothèque Choisie* which was at once generous and judicious. Bentley also received a graceful note from Atterbury, now Dean of Christ Church. "I am indebted to you, Sir," says the Dean, "for the great pleasure and instruction I have received from that excellent performance; though at ye same time I cannot but own to you the uneasyness I felt when I found how many things in Horace there were, which, after thirty years' acquaintance with him, I did not understand." There is much of Horace in that.

CHAPTER IX.

ONE of Bentley's few intimate friends in the second half
of his life was Dr. Richard Mead, an eminent physician,
and in other ways also a remarkable man. After gradu-
ating at the University of Padua—which, as Cambridge
men will remember, had been the second *alma mater* of
Dr. John Caius—Dr. Mead began practice at Stepney in
1696. He rose rapidly to the front rank of his profession,
in which he stood from about 1720 to his death in 1754.
Dibdin describes him with quaint enthusiasm. "His
house was the general receptacle of men of genius and
talent, and of everything beautiful, precious, or rare. His
curiosities, whether books, or coins, or pictures, were laid
open to the public; and the enterprising student and ex-
perienced antiquary alike found amusement and a courteous reception. He was known to all foreigners of intellectual distinction, and corresponded both with the artisan
and the potentate."

In 1721—Bentley being in London at the time—Mead
gave him a copy of a Greek inscription just published by
the accomplished antiquary, Edmund Chishull, who had
been chaplain to the English Factory at Smyrna. A marble slab, about 8 feet 7 inches high and 18 inches broad,

7

had been found in the Troad. It is now in the British
Museum. This slab had supported the bust of a person
who had presented some pieces of plate to the citizens of
Sigeum; on the upper part, an inscription in Ionic Greek
records the gifts; lower down, nearly the same words are
repeated in Attic Greek, with the addition—"Æsopus and
his brothers made me." Bentley dashed off a letter to
Mead; there had been no bust at all, he said; the two inscriptions on the slab were merely copied from two of the
pieces of plate; the artists named were the silversmiths.
He was mistaken. The true solution is clearly that which
has since been given by Kirchhoff. The Ionic inscription
was first carved by order of the donor, a native of the
Ionic Proconnesus; the lower inscription was added at
Sigeum, where settlers had introduced the Attic dialect, on
its being found that the upper inscription could not easily
be read from beneath; Æsopus and his brothers were the
stone-cutters. Yet Bentley's letter incidentally throws a
flash of light on a point not belonging to its main subject.
A colossal statue of Apollo had been dedicated in Delos
by the islanders of Naxos. On the base are these words:
ΟϜΥΤΟΛΙΘΟΕΜΙΑΝΔΡΙΑΣΚΑΙΤΟΣΦΕΛΑΣ. Bentley
read this (τ)οϜυτοῦ [=ταὐτοῦ] λίθου εἴμ', ἀνδριὰς καὶ τὸ
σφέλας, an iambic trimeter (with hiatus): "I am of the
same stone, statue and pedestal."

After this instance of rashness, it is right to record a
striking success. In 1728 Chishull published an inscription from copies made by the travellers Spon and Wheeler.
Bentley, in a private letter, suggested some corrections;
but Chishull, who saw the criticisms without knowing
the author, demurred to some of them, thinking that the
copies could not have been so inexact. Some years later
the stone itself was brought to England. It then appeared

that the copies had been wrong, and that Bentley's conjectural reading agreed in every particular with the marble itself. That marble is in the British Museum: it was found at the ancient Chalcedon on the Bosporus, opposite Constantinople, and had supported a statue of *Zeus Ourios*, *i. e.*, "Zeus the giver of fair winds." He had a famous temple in that neighbourhood, at the mouth of the Black Sea, where voyagers through the straits were wont to make their vows. The inscription (3797 in the *Corpus*) consists of four elegiac couplets, of which the style would justify us in supposing that they were at least as old as the age of Alexander: I translate them:

> "Zeus, the sure guide who sends the favouring gale,
> Claims a last vow before ye spread the sail:
> If to the Azure Rocks your course ye urge,
> Where in the strait Poseidon lifts the surge,
> Or through the broad Ægean seek your home,
> Here lay your gift—and speed across the foam.
> Behold the god, whose wafting breath divine
> All mortals welcome: Philon raised the sign."

It was shortly before his death in 1742 that this proof of his acuteness was given to the world (by John Taylor), along with another. A Persian manuscript bore the date "*Yonane* (Ionian) 1504:" Bentley showed that this was reckoned from the foundation of the dynasty of Seleucidæ —"Ionian" being the general Oriental name for "Hellene"—and meant the year of 1193 of our era.

In 1724 an edition of Terence was published by Dr. Francis Hare. Bentley had long meditated such a work. He was never a jealous man. But he had a good deal of the feeling expressed by the verse, "Shame to be mute and let barbarians speak." He put forth all his powers. At the beginning of 1726—that is, some eighteen months after the appearance of Hare's Terence—Bentley's came out. And it was not Terence only. Hare had promised the Fables of Phœdrus, and Bentley forestalled him by giving these in the same volume; also the "Sentences" (273 lines) of the so-called Publius Syrus.

The Terence is one of Bentley's titles to fame. Any attempt to criticise such an author's text demands a knowledge of his metres. Bentley was the first modern who threw any clear light on the metrical system of the Latin dramatists. Here, as in other cases, it is essential to remember the point at which he took up the work. Little or nothing of scientific value had been done before him. The prevalent view had been based on that of Priscian, who recognised in Terence only two metres, the iambic and the trochaic — the metre of which the basis is $\smile -$, and that of which it is $- \smile$. Every verse was to be forced into one or other of these moulds, by assuming all manner of "licences" on the part of the poet. Nay, Priscian says that in his time some persons denied that there were any metres in Terence at all! ("*Quosdam vel abnegare esse in Terentii comoediis metra.*") In the preface to an edition of Terence which appeared almost simultaneously with Bentley's, the Dutch editor, Westerhof, alludes ironically to a hint in Bentley's Horace (Sat. II. v. 79) that it was possible to restore the Terentian metres; a sneer which it was Westerhof's fate to expiate by compiling the index for Bentley's second edition when it was published at Amsterdam in 1727. The scholars of the sixteenth century who had treated the subject—Glareanus, Erasmus, Faernus—had followed the "licence" theory. Bentley's object was to reclaim as much as possible from this supposed realm of "licence," and enlarge the domain of law. He points out, first, the variety of Terence's metres, and illustrates each by an English verse. He then defines certain metrical differences between Roman Comedy, as in Terence, and Roman epic poetry, as in Virgil. The characteristic of Bentley's views on Terentian metre consisted in taking account of accent ("prosody" in the proper sense), and not solely of quantity. To judge from some of Bentley's emendations in poetry, his ear for sound was not very fine; but his ear for rhythm was exact. Guided by this, he could see that the influence of accent in Roman Comedy sometimes overruled the epic and lyric canons of quantitative metre. In one case, however, his attention to accent led him into an erroneous refinement. In Latin, he says, no word of two or more syllables is accented on the last syllable: thus it is *virum*, not *virúm*. Comic poets, he urges, writing for popular audiences, had to guard as much as possible against laying a metrical stress on these final syllables which could not support an accent. In the iambic trimeter they could not observe this rule everywhere. But Terence, said Bentley, always observes it in the third foot. As an example, I may take this verse:

"Ultro ád | me ven‖it ún|icam ‖ gnatám | suam:"

where the rule, though broken in the 5th foot, is kept in the 3rd. But Bentley seems not to have noticed that this is a result of metre, not of accent: it is due to the caesura.

Bentley corrected the text of Terence in about a thousand places ("mille, opinor, locis," he says)—chiefly on metrical grounds. Yet in every scene of every play, according to Ritschl, he left serious blemishes. That only shows what was the state of the field in which Bentley broke new ground. His work must not be judged as if he propounded a complete metrical doctrine. Rather he threw out a series of original remarks, right in some points, wrong in others, pregnant in all. G. Hermann and Ritschl necessarily speak of Bentley's labours on Terence with mingled praise and censure; both, however, do full justice to the true instinct with which he led the attack on the problem. Modern studies in Latin metre and pronunciation have advanced the questions treated by Bentley to a new stage; but his merit remains. He was the pioneer of metrical knowledge in its application to the Latin drama.

A word of mention is due to the very curious Latin speech which Bentley has printed in his Terence after the sketch of the metres. It was delivered by him on July 6, 1725, when, as Regius Professor of Divinity, he had occasion to present seven incepting doctors in that faculty. He interprets the old symbols of the doctoral degree—the cap—the book—the gold ring—the chair "believe those who have tried it—no bench is so hard") —and congratulates the University on the beneficence of George I. It has been wondered why Bentley inserted this speech in his Terence. Surely the reason is evident. He had recently been restored to those degrees which had been taken from him by the Cambridge Senate in 1718. He seizes this opportunity of intimating to the world that he is once more in full exercise of his functions as Regius Professor of Divinity.

It was in his seventy-seventh year (1739) that Bentley fulfilled a project of his youth by publishing an edition of Manilius. At the age of twenty-nine (1691) he had been. actively collecting materials, and had even made some progress with the text. In 1727 we find that this work, so long laid aside, stood first on the list of prom-

ises to be redeemed : and in 1736 it was ready for press.
A proposal for publishing it was made to Bentley by a
London "Society for the Encouragement of Learning,"
which aimed at protecting authors from booksellers.
Bentley declined. The Manilius was printed in 1739 by
Henry Woodfall. It is a beautiful quarto; the frontispiece is Vertue's engraving of Thornhill's portrait of Bentley, *aetat.* 48 (1710) ; a good engraving, though a con-
ventional benignity tames and spoils that peculiar expression which is so striking in the picture at Trinity College.

Manilius is the author of an epic poem in five books,
called *Astronomica :* but popular astronomy is subordinate, in his treatment, to astrology.   Strangely enough,
the poet's age was so open a question with the scholars
of the seventeenth century that Gevärts actually identi-
fied him with Theodorus Mallius, consul in 399 A.D., whom
Claudian panegyrises. The preface to Bentley's edition,
written by his nephew Richard, rightly assigns Manilius
to the age of Augustus, though without giving the internal proofs. These are plain. Book I. was finished after
the defeat of Varus (A.D. 9), and Book IV. before the
death of Augustus (A.D. 14). F. Jacob, in his edition of
the poet (rec. Berlin 1846), understands a verse in Book
v. (512) as referring to the restoration by Tiberius of
Pompey's Theatre, after it had been burnt down in 22
A.D.   But, according to the marble of Ancyra, Augustus
also had repaired that theatre at a great cost, and took
credit for allowing the name of Pompey to remain in the
dedicatory inscription, instead of replacing it by his own.
Clearly it is to this that the words of Manilius allude—
"*Hinc Pompeia manent veteris monimenta triumphi*"—im-
plying a compliment not only to the munificence, but to
the magnanimity, of Augustus.   There is no reason, then,

for doubting that the whole poem was composed, or took
its present shape, between A.D. 9 and A.D. 14. The poet
gives no clue to his own origin, but his style has a strongly Greek tinge.

Scaliger pronounced him "equal in sweetness to Ovid,
and superior in majesty;" a verdict which Bentley cites
with approval. To most readers it will be scarcely intel-
ligible. Where Manilius deals with the technical parts
of astronomy, he displays, indeed, excellent ingenuity;
but, in the frequent passages where he imitates Lucretius,
the contrast between a poet and a rhetorician is made
only more glaring by an archaic diction. The episode of
Andromeda and Perseus, in his fifth book, and a passage
on human reason in the second, were once greatly admired.
To show him at his best, however, I should rather take
one of those places where he expresses more simply a feeling of wonder and awe common to every age. "Where-
fore see we the stars arise in their seasons, and move, as
at a word spoken, on the paths appointed for them? Of
whom there is none that hastens, neither is there any that
tarries behind. Why are the summer nights beautiful
with these that change not, and the nights of winter from
of old? These things are not the work of chance, but the
order of a God most high."

Bentley's treatment of the text sometimes exhibits all
his brilliancy: thus in Book v. 737 the received text had—

> "Sic etiam magno quaedam respondere mundo
> *Haec* Natura facit, quae *caeli* condidit orbem."

This *respondĕre* had even been quoted to show that the
poem was post-classical. The MSS. have not *Haec*, but
QUAM; not *caeli*, but CAELO; and one good MS. has MUN-
DO EST. Bentley restores:

> " Sic etiam in magno quaedam RESPUBLICA mundo est,
>   Quam Natura facit, quae caelo condidit URBEM."

" So also in the great firmament there is a commonwealth, wrought by Nature, who hath ordered a city in the heavens." *Respondere* arose from a contraction *resp.* And *urbem* is made certain by the next verses, which elaborate the comparison of the starry hierarchy to the various ranks of civic life. But this, Bentley's last published work, shows a tendency from which his earlier criticism was comparatively free. Not content with amending, he rejects very many verses as spurious. The total number is no less than 170 out of 4220 lines which the poem contains. In the vast majority of cases, the ground of rejection is wholly and obviously inadequate. As an example of his rashness here, we may take one passage—which, I venture to think, he has not understood. At the beginning of Book IV. Manilius is reciting the glories of Rome :

> " Quid referam Cannas admotaque moenibus arma ?
>   Varronemque fuga magnum (quod vivere possit
>   Postque tuos, Thrasimene, lacus) Fabiumque morando ?
>   *Accepisse iugum victas Carthaginis arces ?*"

"Why should I tell of Cannæ, and of (Carthaginian) arms carried to the walls of Rome? Why tell of Varro, great in his flight, . . . and Fabius, in his delay? Or how the conquered towers of Carthage received our yoke ?"

Varro's " flight " is his escape from the field of Cannæ, after which he saved the remnant of the Roman army. The words, " *quod vivere possit Postque tuos, Thrasimene, lacus,*" are untranslatable. Bentley seems to have understood : " in that he can live, and that, too, after the battle at Lake Thrasimene ;" but, to say no more, *que* forbids this. And then he rejects the whole line, " *Accepisse—*

7*

arces." Why? Because "yokes" are put on peoples,
not on "towers!" Now the oldest manuscript (Gembla-
censis) has not *vivere*, but VINCERE: the MSS. have not
quod (a conjecture), but QUAM. They have also MORAN-
TEM (not *morando*), VICTAE (not *victas*). I should read:

> "Quid referam Cannas admotaque moenibus arma?
> Varronemque fuga magnum, Fabiumque morantem?
> Postque tuos, Thrasimene, lacus QUOM VINCERE POSSET,
> Accepisse iugum victae Carthaginis arces?"

"and that—though after the fight by thy waters, Thrasimene, she
could hope to conquer—the towers of conquered Carthage received
our yoke."

The words "quom vincere posset" allude to the imminent peril of Rome after Hannibal's great victory at Lake
Thrasimene, when the fall of the city seemed inevitable if
the conqueror should march upon it. (Cp. Liv. XXII. 7 f.)

It remains to speak of another labour which Bentley
was not destined to complete, but which, even in its comparatively slight relics, offers points of great interest—his
Homer.

The first trace of Homeric criticism by Bentley occurs
in a letter which he wrote to his friend Davies, of Queens'
College, just after Joshua Barnes had published his edition of the Iliad and Odyssey (1711). Barnes, who was
unreasonably offended with Bentley, refers in his preface
to a certain "hostile person," a very Zoilus. "If he mean
me," says Bentley, "I have but dipped yet into his notes,
and yet I find everywhere just occasion of censure."
Bentley then shows that Barnes had made an arbitrary
change in a line of the Iliad (αὐτάρ for ἀλλά in XIV. 101),
through not seeing that a reading which had stood in all
former editions, and which had puzzled the Greek com-

mentator Eustathius, was a mere blunder (ἀποπτανέουσιν for ἀποπαπτανέουσιν). In 1713 Bentley published his "Remarks" on the "Discourse of Free-thinking" by Anthony Collins. Collins had spoken of the Iliad as "the epitome of all arts and sciences," adding that Homer "designed his poem for eternity, to please and instruct mankind." "Take my word for it," says Bentley, "poor Homer, in those circumstances and early times, had never such aspiring thoughts. He wrote a sequel of songs and rhapsodies, to be sung by himself for small earnings and good cheer, at festivals and other days of merriment; the *Ilias* he made for the men, and the *Odysseïs* for the other sex. These loose songs were not collected together in the form of an epic poem till Pisistratus's time, above [2nd edition: 1st, *about*] 500 years after." There is some ambiguity in the phrase, "a *sequel* of songs and rhapsodies." It seems improbable that Bentley meant, "a *connected* series."

When Bentley wrote this, the origin of the Homeric poems had not yet become a subject of modern controversy. It would be unfair to press his casual utterance as if it were a carefully defined statement. Yet it is interesting to note the general outlines of the belief which satisfied a mind so bold and so acute. He supposes, then, that a poet named Homer lived about 1050 B.C. This poet "wrote" (by which, perhaps, he meant no more than "composed") both the Iliad and the Odyssey. But neither of them was given to the world by Homer as a single epic. Each consisted of many short lays, which Homer recited separately. These lays circulated merely as detached pieces, until they were collected about 550 B.C. into the two epics which we possess.

Seventy-two years later F. A. Wolf published his *Prol-*

egomena. The early epic poetry of Greece, Wolf argues, was transmitted by oral recitation, not by writing. But *our* Iliad and Odyssey could not have been composed without writing. We must conclude, then, that the Homeric poems were originally, in Bentley's phrase, "a sequel of songs and rhapsodies." These "loose songs" were first written down and arranged by the care of Peisistratus. Thus Bentley's sentence contains the germ of the view which Wolf developed. Yet it would be an error to conceive Bentley here as an original sceptic, who threw out the first pregnant hint of a new theory. Bentley's relation to the modern Homeric question is of a different kind. The view which he expresses was directly derived by him from notices in ancient writers; as when Pausanias says that the Homeric poems, before their collection by Peisistratus, had been "scattered, and preserved only by memory, some here, some there." Cicero, Plutarch, Diogenes Laertius, the Platonic *Hipparchus*, Heracleides Ponticus, were other witnesses to whom Bentley could appeal.

He brought forward and approved that old tradition at a time when the original unity of each epic was the received belief. It was not till the latter part of the eighteenth century that the passion for returning from "art" to "nature" prepared a welcome for the doctrine that the Iliad and the Odyssey are parcels of primitive folk-songs. But then we note the off-hand way in which Bentley's statement assumes points which have since vexed Homeric research. He assumes that the Iliad and Odyssey are made up of parts which were *originally* intended for detached recitations: an inference to which the structure of the poems is strongly adverse. He accepts without reserve the tradition regarding Peisistratus. By the ancient saying that the Iliad was written for men and the Odys-

sey for women, Bentley probably understood no more
than that the Iliad deals with war, and the Odyssey with
the trials of a true wife.   There is, indeed, a further sense
in which we might say that the Iliad, with its historical
spirit, was masculine, and the Odyssey, with its fairy-land
wonders and its tender pathos, more akin to *das Ewigwei-
bliche;* but we cannot read that meaning into Bentley's
words.   He seems to have found no such difference between the characters of the two epics as constrained him
to become a " separator."   He had not felt, what is now
so generally admitted, that the Odyssey bears the marks
of a later time than the Iliad.   Briefly, then, we cannot
properly regard Bentley as a forerunner of the Homeric
controversy on its literary or historical side, pre-eminently
as his critical gifts would have fitted him to take up the
question.   He knew the ancient sources on which Wolf
afterwards worked, but he had not given his mind to sifting them.   Bentley's connexion with Homeric criticism
is wholly on the side of the text, and chiefly in regard to
metre.

In 1726 Bentley was meditating an edition of Homer,
but intended first to finish his labours on the New Testament.   In 1732 he definitely committed himself to the
Homeric task.   At that time the House of Lords had before it the question whether the Bishop of Ely could try
Bentley.   As the Horace had been dedicated to Harley, so
the Homer was to be dedicated to Lord Carteret, a peer
who was favourable to the Master of Trinity's cause, and
who encouraged the design by granting or procuring the
loan of manuscripts.   In 1734 we find Bentley at work
on Homer.   But, though he made some progress, nothing
was published.   Trinity College possesses the only relics
of his Homeric work.

First, there is a copy of H. Estienne's folio *Poetae Graeci*. In this Bentley had read through the Iliad, Odyssey, and Homeric Hymns, writing very brief notes in the margin, which are either his own corrections, or readings from manuscripts or grammarians. In the Hymns the notes become rarer; and it is evident that all were written rapidly. This is the book which Trinity College sent in 1790 to Göttingen, for the use of Heyne, who warmly acknowledges the benefit in the preface to his edition of the Iliad. Secondly, a small quarto manuscript book contains somewhat fuller notes by Bentley on the first six books of the Iliad. These notes occupy 43 pages of the book, ceasing abruptly at verse 54 of Iliad VII. Lastly, there is the manuscript draft of Bentley's notes on the digamma, the substance of which has been published by J. W. Donaldson in his *New Cratylus*.

The distinctive feature of Bentley's Homeric work is the restoration of the digamma. Bentley's discovery was too much in advance of his age to be generally received otherwise than with ridicule or disbelief. Even F. A. Wolf, who yielded to few in his admiration of the English critic, could speak of the digamma as merely an illusion which, in old age, mocked the genius of Bentley (*senile ludibrium ingenii Bentleiani*). At the present day, when the philological fact has so long been seen in a clearer light, it is easy to underrate the originality and the insight which the first perception of it showed.

In reading Homer, Bentley had been struck by such things as these. The words, "*and Atreides the king*," are in Homer, *Atreides te anax*. Now the *e* in *te* would naturally be cut off before the first *a* in *anax*, making *t'anax*. But the poet cannot have meant to cut it off, since that would spoil the metre. Why, then, was he able to avoid

cutting it off? Because, said Bentley, in Homer's time
the word *anax* did not begin with a vowel: it was *vanax*.
Many old writers mention a letter which had disappeared
from the ordinary Greek alphabet. Its sound had been
like the Latin v—that is, probably, like our w. Its form
was like F: which, to Greek eyes, suggested their letter
gamma, Γ, with another gamma on its shoulders: and so
they called this F the "double gamma," the *digamma*.
Several words are specified by the old grammarians as
having once begun with this digamma. Bentley tried the
experiment of replacing it before such words where they
occurred in Homer. Very often, he found, this explained a gap (or "hiatus"), like that in *Atreides te anax*. He
came to the conclusion that, when the Homeric poems
were composed, this letter was still used, and that it should
always be prefixed, in Homer, to those words which once
had it.

The first hint of this idea occurs in Bentley's copy (now
at Trinity College) of the "Discourse of Free-thinking"
by Anthony Collins, which Bentley was reading and an-
notating in 1713. On a blank leaf at the end he has
written:

"Homer's δίγαμμα Aeolicum to be added. οἶνος, Ϝοῖνος, vinū: a
Demonstration of this, because Ϝοῖνος has always preceding it a
vowel: so οἰνοποτάζων."

Bentley's view was noticed by his friend Dr. Samuel
Clarke, in the second volume of his Iliad, published post-
humously in 1732. In the same year came forth Bentley's edition of *Paradise Lost*, in which he had occasion to quote Homer. There the digamma makes its
modern *début* in all the majesty of a capital F—for which
printers now use the sign Ϝ. It was the odd look of such

a word as Ϝέτος that inspired Pope with the lines in the
Dunciad. Bentley speaks:

> "Roman and Greek grammarians! know your better,
>   Author of something yet more great than letter;
>   While tow'ring o'er your alphabet, like Saul,
>   Stands our digamma, and o'ertops them all."

Bentley had thrown a true and brilliant light on the
text of Homer. But, as was natural then, he pushed his
conclusion too far. The Greek *Ϝoinos* is the same as
vinum and *wine*. Homer, Bentley thought, could no
more have said *oinos*, instead of *voinos*, than Romans
could say *inum*, or Englishmen *ine*. Accordingly, he set
to work to restore this letter all through the Homeric
poems. Often it mended the metre, but not seldom it
marred it; and then Bentley was for changing the text.
A single instance will give some idea of his task. In Iliad
I. 202 we have the words *hŭbrĭn ĭdē* (ὕβριν ἴδῃ), (that thou
mayest) "see the insolence." This word *ide* was originally
vide: its stem *vid* is that of the Latin *video* and our *wit*.
Homer, said Bentley, could have written nothing but *vide*.
And so, to make the metre right, he reads a different word
(ὀρῇς). Now let us see what this involves. This stem
vid is the parent of several words, very frequent in Homer, for *seeing, seeming, knowing, form*, etc. On Bentley's
view, every one of these must always, in Homer, begin
with Ϝ. The number of changes required can easily be
estimated by any one who will consult Prendergast's Con-
cordance to the Iliad, Dunbar's to the Odyssey and Homeric Hymns. I do not guarantee the absolute precision
of the following numbers, but they are at least approximately correct. I find that about 832 derivatives of the
stem *vid* occur in the Iliad, Odyssey, and Hymns. By Ϝ

I denote those cases in which the metre *requires* the digamma: by N, those in which the metre *excludes* it: by Q, those cases which prove nothing:

	Total.	Ϝ	N	Q
Iliad	357	205	81	71
Odyssey. . .	376	220	76	80
Hymns . . .	99	38	34	27
	832	463	191	178

So, for this one root *vid*, Bentley would have been compelled to amend the text of Homer in about 191 places. The number of digammated roots in Homer is between 30 and 40; no other is so prolific as *vid;* but a consistent restoration of the digamma would require change in at least several hundreds of places; and often under conditions which require that the changes, if any, should be extremely bold.   Bentley's error consisted in regarding the digamma as a constant element, like any other letter in the radical parts of the words to which it had once been prefixed.   It was not this, but rather the ghost of a vanished letter, which, in Homeric metre, fitfully haunts its ancient seats.   Nor is it the only such ghost.   When Bentley found that, in Homer, the word ὡς, "as," can be treated as if it began with a consonant, he wrote Ϝὡς: but the lost initial was not the spirant v: it was y: for ὡς is merely the ablative of ὅ-ς, the Sanskrit *yât*.

Apart from the restoration of the digamma, the relics of Bentley's work on Homer present other attempts at emendation.   These are always acute and ingenious; but the instances are rare indeed in which they would now

commend themselves to students. I give a few specimens
below, in order that scholars may judge of their general
character.* The boldness with which Bentley was disposed to correct Homer may be illustrated by a single example. Priam, the aged king of Troy, is standing beside
Helen on the walls, and looking forth on the plain where
warriors are moving. He sees Odysseus passing along
the ranks of his followers, and asks Helen who that is.
"His arms lie on the earth that feedeth many: but he

---

* I. *From Bentley's MS. notes in the margin of the Homer.*

Odyssey I. 23 ('Αλλ' ὁ μὲν Αἰθίοπας μετεκίαθε τηλόθ' ἐόντας, |
Αἰθίοπας, τοὶ διχθὰ δεδαίαται, ἔσχατοι ἀνδρῶν). "legendum Αἰθίοπες:
si vera lectio Il. Z. 396." (θυγάτηρ μεγαλήτορος Ἡετίωνος, | Ἡετίων,
ὅς ἔναιεν, κ.τ.λ.) [Lucian speaks of "Attic solecisms"—deliberate
imitations, by late writers, of the irregular grammar found in Attic writers: surely this is a gratuitous "Homeric solecism."] 29.
(μνήσατο γὰρ κατὰ θυμὸν ἀμύμονος Αἰγίσθοιο) Bentley conjectures
κατὰ νοῦν ἀνύμονος. 51. θεὰ δ' ἐν δώμασι ναίει "Eust. not. ἐν
δώματα ναίει pro vulg. δώμασι, sed lego θεὰ δ' ἐν πότνια ναίει. ἐνναίει
absolute, ut ἐνναίουσι Il. I. 154, 296. Sic Od. E. 215 eam compellens
Πότνα θεά. κοὐ δώματα ἔναιεν sed σπέος. Ibidem." [*i. e.*, Bentley
objects to the word δώματα because Calypso lived in a cave. But
ἐν δώματα ναίει is unquestionably right.]

II. *From his MS. book of notes on Iliad* I.–VII. 54.

Iliad III. 46 ἢ τοιόσδε ἐών. Amabant, credo, Hiatus; non solum
tolerabant. Dedit poeta ἢ τοιοῦτος ἐών. 212. (μύθους καὶ μήδεα
πᾶσιν ὕφαινον.) Casaubonus ad Theocritum c. IX. corrigit ἔφαινον.
Recte. ἔφαινον μύθους, in concione loquebantur. Sic Il. σ. 295,
Νήπιε, μηκέτι ταῦτα νοήματα φαῖν' ἐνὶ δήμῳ. 357. (διὰ μὲν ἀσπίδος
ἦλθε φαεινῆς ὄβριμον ἔγχος.) Saepe redit hic versiculus qui si vere
ab Homero est, Licentia nescio qua pronuntiabitur Δῖα μὲν, ut Ἄρες,
Ἄρες. Non enim tribrachys pro Dactylo hic ponitur ad exprimendam
Hastae celeritatem, non magis quam Molossus pes trium longarum ad
tarditatem exprimendam. Quid si legat quis, Διαπρὸ μὲν, pede Pro-
celeusmatico, ut "capitibu' nutantes pinus," "Parietibus textum
caecis iter."

himself, like a leader of the flock (κτίλος ὥς), moves along
the ranks of men; yea, I liken him to a young ram with
thick fleece, that passeth through a great flock of white
sheep." Bentley, thinking that ὥς must be Ϝώς, had to
get rid of κτίλος somehow. "Never yet," says Bentley,
"have I seen a ram ordering the ranks of men. And
what tautology! He moves along, like a ram: and I compare him to a ram!" And so he changes the ram into a
word meaning "unarmed" (writing αὐτὰρ ψιλὸς ἐὼν instead of αὐτὸς δὲ κτίλος ὥς), because the arms of Odysseus
are said to be lying on the ground.

Bentley had done first-rate work on some authors who
would have rewarded him better than Homer—better than
Horace or Manilius. It was his habit to enter collations
of manuscripts, or his own conjectures, in the margins of
his classical books. Some of these books are at Cambridge. Many more are in the British Museum. The
Gentleman's Magazine for 1807 relates how Kidd found
60 volumes, formerly Bentley's, at the London bookseller
Lackington's, to whom they had been sold by Cumberland, and from whom they were at once bought for the
Museum by the Trustees. The complete list of the Bentley books in the British Museum comprises (omitting
duplicates) 70 works. All, or nearly all, the manuscript
notes which enrich these volumes have now been printed
somewhere. The notes on Lucan, whom Bentley had intended to edit, were published by Cumberland in 1760.
Among the most ingenious emendations are those on Nicander, the Greek physician of Colophon (*circ.* 150 B.C.),
whose epic on venomous bites (*Theriaca*) Bentley had an-
notated at the request of Dr. Mead. But the province of
Greek and Roman literature in which these remains most
strikingly illustrate Bentley's power is, on the whole, that
of the comic drama.

He had sent Küster his remarks on two plays of Aristophanes—the *Plutus* and *Clouds*. All the eleven comedies have his marginal notes in his copy of Froben's
edition, now in the British Museum. These notes were
first published by G. Burges in the *Classical Journal*, xi.–
xiv. For exact scholarship, knowledge, and brilliant felicity, they are wonderfully in advance of anything which had
then been done for the poet. Porson is said to have felt
the joy of a truly great scholar on finding that his own
emendations of Aristophanes had been anticipated, in some
seventy instances, by the predecessor whom he so highly
revered. Bentley's emendations of Plautus are also very
remarkable. They have been published, for the first time,
by Mr. E. A. Sonnenschein, in his edition of the *Captivi*
(1880), from the Plautus in the British Museum which
Bentley used; it is the second edition of Pareus (Frank-
furt, 1623). All our twenty comedies have been touched
more or less—the number of Bentley's conjectures in each
ranging from perhaps 20 to 150 or more.

As in Aristophanes, so in Plautus, Bentley sometimes
anticipated the best thoughts of later critics. Such coin-
cidences show how much he was in advance of his age.
Those conjectures of Bentley's which were afterwards
made independently by such men as Porson or Ritschl
were in most cases *certain;* in Bentley's day, however,
they were as yet beyond the reach of every one else. Nor
must we overlook his work on Lucretius. That library of
Isaac Voss which Bentley had vainly sought to secure for
Oxford carried with it to Leyden the two most important
MSS. of Lucretius—one of the 9th century (Munro's A),
another of the 10th (B). Bentley had to work without
these. His notes—first completely published in the Glasgow edition of Wakefield (1813) — fill only 22 octavo

pages in the Oxford edition of 1818. But their quality
has been recognised by the highest authority. Munro
thinks that Bentley, if he had had the Leyden MSS.,
"might have anticipated what Lachmann did by a century and a half." Another labour also, in another field,
descended from Bentley to Lachmann: of that we must
now speak.

CHAPTER X.

THE PROPOSED EDITION OF THE NEW TESTAMENT.

Dr. John Mill published in 1707 his edition of the Greek Testament, giving in foot-notes the various readings which he had collected by the labour of thirty years. To understand the impression which this work produced, it is necessary to recall the nature of its predecessors. The Greek text of the New Testament, as then generally read, was ultimately based on two sixteenth century editions; that of Erasmus (Basel, 1516), which had been marked by much carelessness; and that due chiefly to Stunica, in the "Complutensian" Polyglott (so called from *Complūtum*, or Alcalá de Henares) of Cardinal Ximenes, printed in 1514, and probably published in 1522. The folio edition printed by Robert Estienne at Paris in 1550 was founded on the text of Erasmus. The Elzevir editions, of which the first appeared in 1624, gave the text of Estienne as imperfectly revised by the reformer Beza. The second Elzevir edition (1633) declared this to be "the text now received by all." Hence it came to be known as the "Received Text."

The existence of various readings, though a well-known, was hardly a prominent fact. Some had been given in the margin of the folio Estienne; Beza had referred to others; more had been noticed by Walton in the Greek

Testament of his Polyglott (1657), and by Bishop Fell in his small edition (1675). The sources of textual evidence generally had been described and discussed with intelligence and candour by the French scholar Simon (1689–95). But Mill's edition was the first which impressed the public mind by marshalling a great array of variants, roughly estimated at thirty thousand. In his learned *Prolegomena* Mill often expressed opinions and preferences, but without supplying any general clue to the labyrinth exhibited in his critical notes.

The alarm felt in some quarters is strikingly shown by Whitby's censure of Mill's edition (1710), in which he goes so far as to affirm that the "Received Text" can be defended *in all places* where the sense is affected (*in iis omnibus locis* lectionem textus defendi posse), and that even in matters "of lesser moment" it is "most rarely" invalidated. On the other hand, anti-Christian writers did not fail to make capital of a circumstance which they represented as impugning the tradition. Thus Anthony Collins, in his "Discourse of Free-thinking," specially dwelt on Mill's 30,000 variants. In his published reply to Collins (1713), Bentley pointed out that such variants are perfectly compatible with the absence of any essential corruption, while he insisted on the value of critical studies in their application to the Scriptures. Dr. Hare, in publicly thanking Bentley for this reply, urged him to undertake an edition of the New Testament. Undoubtedly there was a wide-spread feeling that some systematic effort should be made towards disengaging a standard text from the variations set forth by Mill.

Three years later (1716), Bentley received a visit from John James Wetstein, a Swiss, related to the Amsterdam publishers who had reprinted Bentley's Horace. Wetstein was then on leave of absence from his duties as a chaplain in the Dutch army. For years he had devoted himself with rare ardour to those critical studies of the New Testament which were afterwards embodied in his edition (1751–2). He had recently collated some Greek MSS. in the Library of Paris. "On hearing this," Wetstein writes, Bentley "urged me to publish my collations, with his aid. I pleaded my youth, and the shortness of my leave of absence; I asked him to undertake the work himself, and to use my collections. At length I moved the great critic to entertain a design of which he seemed to have had no thought before—that of editing the New Testament."

It is assumed by Tregelles that Wetstein was mistaken in supposing that Bentley had not previously contemplated an edition. Bentley's *studies* on the New Testament dated, it is true, from his earliest manhood; there are traces of them in his Letter to Mill (1691), no less than in his reply to Collins; he had already collated the Alexandrine MS., and had been using the "Codex Bezae" (his "Cantabrigiensis," belonging to the University Library) since 1715. But it does not follow that Wetstein's statement is not accurate. The fact that Bentley was deeply studying a subject is never sufficient to prove that he meant to write upon it.

Now, at any rate, the plan was definitely formed, and Wetstein returned to Paris, in order to aid it by further collations. In April, 1716, Bentley announced his project in a remarkable letter to the Archbishop of Canterbury, Dr. Wake. Monk hints, though he does not say, that Bentley's object was "to interest the public," in view of imminent law proceedings. I quite agree with Mr. A. A. Ellis, the editor of *Bentleii Critica Sacra*, that in this case there is no real ground for such a suggestion. Bentley's enthusiasm for the work was sincere, as his correspondence with Wetstein abundantly shows; he did not bring his scheme before the public till 1720; and his object in addressing the Primate was no other than that which he states, viz., to learn whether the project was likely to be encouraged. After sketching his plan, he observes to Dr. Wake that it might be made forever impossible by a fire in the Royal Library of Paris or London. It is startling to read this foreboding, expressed in 1716. Fifteen years later, a fire actually broke out at night in the King's Library, then lodged at Abingdon House, Westminster— when the Cottonian Genesis was seriously damaged. An eye-witness of the scene has described Bentley hurrying out of the burning Library, in his night-gown and his great wig, with the most precious of his charges, the Alexandrine manuscript of the Greek Bible, under his arm.

The Archbishop's reply to Bentley is not extant, but appears to have been favourable. For the next four years (1716–20) Bentley continued to gather materials. Wetstein was not his only ally. David Casley, the Deputy King's Librarian, worked for him in the libraries of Oxford. More important still was the aid of John Walker, a Fellow of Trinity College, who went to Paris in 1719, and passed nearly a year there in collating manuscripts. Walker was most kindly received by the Benedictines of St. Maur, with whom Bentley had already been placed in communication by Wetstein. They provided him with a room in their monastery at St. Germain des Prés, procured collations from the Benedictines of Angers, and personally aided his work in their own library.

Walker returned from Paris in 1720. Bentley now

8

published his "Proposals for Printing," in which he explains the principles of his edition. He observes that the printed texts of the New Testament, Greek and Latin, are based on comparatively recent manuscripts. His aim has been to recover from older Latin manuscripts the text of the Latin "Vulgate" as formed by Jerome [about 383 A.D.], and to compare this with the oldest Greek manuscripts. Jerome's version was not only strictly literal, but aimed at representing the very order of the Greek words. Where it agrees with our oldest Greek manuscripts, there, Bentley argues, we may recognise the Greek text as received by the Church at the time of the Council of Nice (325 A.D.) "and two centuries after." This test will set aside about four-fifths of those 30,000 various readings which "crowd the pages" of the editions. The text of the New Testament can be fixed "to the smallest nicety." As corroborative evidence, Bentley further proposes to use the Syriac, Coptic, Gothic, and Æthiopic versions (in which Walton's Polyglott would help him), and the citations by the Greek and Latin Fathers, within the first five centuries. Those centuries are to be the limit of the various readings which his foot-notes will exhibit. And he reassures the public mind on a point which might well occasion uneasiness. "The author is very sensible, that in the Sacred Writings there's no place for conjectures or emendations." He will not "alter one letter in the text" without the authorities given in the notes, but will relegate conjectural criticism to the *Prolegomena*. The work is to be "a Charter, a Magna Charta, to the whole Christian Church; to last when all the ancient MSS. here quoted may be lost and extinguished." As a specimen of his edition, Bentley subjoined the last chapter of Revelation, with notes supporting those readings which he restores to the text, whilst the "received" readings, when displaced, are given in the margin.

The "Proposals" had scarcely appeared when they were anonymously attacked by Dr. Conyers Middleton, who was then in the midst of his feud with Bentley. This was the year of the South Sea scheme, and Dr. Middleton allowed himself to write of "Bentley's Bubble." Bentley's reply—founded on the supposition that his assailant was Colbatch—was still more deplorable. Middleton then printed, with his name, "Some Further Remarks," criticising the "Proposals" more in detail, and on some points with force. Colbatch writes to Middleton: "According to all that I can speak with or hear from, you have laid Bentley flat upon his back." Bentley writes to Atterbury (now Bishop of Rochester): "I scorn to read the rascal's book; but if your Lordship will send me any part which you think the strongest, I will undertake to answer it before night."

Meanwhile the public subscription invited by the "Proposals" already amounted, in 1721, to two thousand pounds. Amidst many distractions, Bentley was certainly continuing to digest his materials. At some time before August, 1726, he received a most important accession to them. The "Vatican" manuscript—which contains the Greek Testament in capital letters as far as the middle of Hebrews ix.—was collated for Bentley by an Italian named Mico. Thomas Bentley, the nephew, being at Rome in 1726, tested Mico's work in three chapters, but did not, as has been supposed, make a complete independent collation. Subsequently the Vaticanus was again collated for Bentley, so far as concerned traces of hands other than "the first," by the Abbé Rulotta, whose services were procured by the Baron de Stosch, then employed in

Italy by the British Government to watch the Pretender.
Rulotta's collation reached Bentley in July, 1729. Its
accuracy, as compared with that of Angelo Mai, was recognised by Tischendorf, when he saw it at Trinity College in 1855. In that same summer of 1729 Bentley
was making inquiries regarding a manuscript, in the Library of the University of Dublin, which contains the
text of the three witnesses (1 John v. 7, 8): it is that
which is known, from the name of the donor, as the Codex Montfortianus, and is not older than the fifteenth
century. Considerable uneasiness appears to have been
felt, after the issue of Bentley's "Proposals," at the prospect of his omitting that text, against which he had decided in his lost dissertation in 1717. It is unnecessary
to remind readers that more recent criticism has finally
rejected the words, for which there is no evidence in
Latin before at least the latter part of the fifth century,
and none in any other language before the fourteenth.

Here—in the summer of 1729—it has usually been
said, as by Monk, that all vestige of the proposed edition
ends. A slight but interesting trace, however, carries us
three years further. From a marginal note in a copy of
the quarto New Testament at Geneva (1620), preserved
in the Wake collection at Christ Church, Oxford, it appears that John Walker was still making collations in
1732. These, it cannot be doubted, were auxiliary to
Bentley's edition, for which the "Proposals" designate
Walker as "overseer and corrector of the press." Seven
years more of working life remained to Bentley, before
the paralytic seizure which overtook him in 1739. Why
was his edition never completed and published? We
need not pause on the curiously inadequate reason suggested by Wetstein—that Bentley resented the refusal of

the Government to remit the duty on foreign paper which
he desired to import. The dates alone refute that, for
the incident occurred in 1721. Probably the answer is
to be sought in a combination of two principal causes—
the worry of litigation which harassed him from 1729 to
1738; and a growing sense of complexity in the problem
of the text, especially after he became better acquainted
with the Vatican readings.

Bentley's materials were bequeathed by him to his
nephew Richard, possibly in the hope that they might be
edited and published. Nothing was done, however. Dr.
Richard Bentley returned the subscriptions, and at his
death in 1786 bequeathed his uncle's collections to Trinity College, where they have since been preserved. Several volumes contain the collations made by Bentley himself or by his various assistants—including Mico's and
Rulotta's collations of the Vaticanus. The point which
Bentley's critical work had reached is best shown by a
folio copy of the Greek and Latin Vulgate (Paris, "apud
Claudium Sonnium," 1628). "Having interleaved it"—
he writes to Wetstein—"I have made my essay of restoring both text and version [i. e., both Greek and Latin];
and they agree and tally even to a miracle; but there
will be (as near as I can guess) near 6000 variations, great
and little, from the received Greek and Latin exemplars."
The notes on the interleaved pages are in Bentley's handwriting from the beginning to the end of the New Testament. He used this volume as a general register of results obtained by his collations—the readings of the Vaticanus, which came to him after nearly all the rest, being
added in paler ink. It is from this folio that Mr. Ellis
prints (besides excerpts) the whole of the Epistle to the
Galatians, in his *Bentleii Critica Sacra* (1862); though it

is to be observed that we cannot assume Bentley's final
acceptance of the text, as there printed, except in the
points on which he has expressly touched. The notes on
Revelation xxii. stand in the folio *verbatim* as they were
printed in the "Proposals" of 1720. Speaking generally
of the work exhibited by the folio, we may say that its
leading characteristics are two—wealth of patristic cita-
tion, and laborious attention to the order of words. It
may further be observed that there does not appear to be
any trace of that confident temerity by which Bentley's
treatment of the classics was so often marked. Had his
edition been published, the promise made in the "Proposals" would, in all probability, have been strictly kept.
Conjectural criticisms would have been confined to the
Prolegomena.

A question of great interest remains. What was the
value of the principle on which Bentley founded his design, and how far has that principle been fruitful in later
work? Bentley's undertaking (as briefly defined in his
letter to Dr. Wake) was, "to give an edition of the Greek
Testament exactly as it was in the best exemplars at the
time of the Council of Nice" (325 A.D.). He saw that,
for this, our ultimate witnesses are the Greek manuscripts
nearest in age to that time. But it might still be asked:
How can we be sure that these oldest Greek manuscripts
represent a text *generally received* at the time when they
were written? Bentley replied: I compare them with
the oldest received Latin translation that I can find. Such
a received Latin version must have represented a received
Greek text. Where it confirms our oldest Greek manuscripts, there is the strongest evidence that their text is
not merely ancient, but also is that text which the Church
received at the time when the Latin version was made.

The evidence of the Fathers, and of ancient versions other than Latin, may help to confirm the proof.

These, then, are the two features of Bentley's conception: the appeal from recent documents to *antiquity*— viz., to the first five centuries; and the appeal to *Greek and Latin consent.*

In the particular application of these ideas Bentley laboured under certain disadvantages which were either almost or altogether inseparable from the time at which he worked. First, it was then scarcely possible that he should adequately realise the history of the Greek text previous to his chosen date, the Council of Nice. The Alexandrine manuscript, of the fifth century, containing the whole of the New Testament in Greek capital letters, had been presented to Charles I. by Cyril Lucar, the Patriarch of Constantinople, in 1628. This was believed to be, as Bentley calls it, " the oldest and best in the world." It was regarded as the typical ancient manuscript, not only by the earlier English editors, Walton, Fell, and Mill, but by Bengel in his edition of 1734. This view has since been modified by data, some of which were not then available. Not less than two or three generations before the Council of Nice (325 A.D.), according to the more recent investigations, two influential types of text had already diverged from the apostolic original. These have been called the " Western " and the "Alexandrian." Both are "Pre-Syrian"—to use the convenient term adopted by Dr. Westcott and Dr. Hort—in distinction from the "*Syrian*" Greek text formed at Antioch at some time between 250 and 350 A.D. The "Syrian" text was eclectic, drawing on both the aberrant Pre-Syrian types, "Western" and "Alexandrian," as well as on texts independent of those two aberrations. In a revised form the Syrian text finally prevailed; a result due partly to the subsequent contraction of Greek Christendom, partly to its centralisation at Constantinople, the ecclesiastical daughter of Antioch.

Four manuscripts of the "uncial" class (written in capitals, as distinguished from "cursive") stand out as the oldest Greek copies of the New Testament. Two belong probably to the middle of the fourth century. One of these is the Vatican manuscript, of which Bentley had no detailed knowledge at the time when he published his "Proposals." Its text is Pre-Syrian, and thus far unique, that in most parts it is free from both Western and Alexandrian corruptions. The other fourth century manuscript is the Sinaitic, of which the New Testament portion first came into Tischendorf's hands in 1859. This also is Pre-Syrian, but with elements both Western and Alexandrian. The Codex Alexandrinus, which Bentley's age deemed the oldest and best, is fundamentally Syrian in the Gospels: in the other books it is still partially Syrian, though Pre-Syrian readings, Western and Alexandrian included, are proportionally more numerous. Thus it contains throughout at least one disturbing element which is absent from the Sinaitic, and at least three which in most of the books are absent from the Vaticanus. The fourth of the oldest uncials is one which Wetstein twice collated at Paris for Bentley—that known as the Codex Ephraemi, because some writings attributed to Ephraem Syrus have been traced over the New Testament. It is coeval with the Alexandrinus, belonging to the fifth century; and, while partly Syrian, it also contains much derived from the earlier texts. In addition to the general but erroneous belief as to the unique value of the Alexandrine manuscript, a singular accident (noticed by Dr. Hort) must have greatly strengthened Bentley's belief in the decisiveness of the agreement between that document and the Vulgate. Jerome, in preparing the Vulgate, appears to have used a Greek manuscript which happened to have many peculiar readings in common with the Alexandrinus, and to have been partly derived from the same original.

The reader will now be able to imagine the effect which must have been gradually wrought on Bentley's mind, as he came to know the Vaticanus better. With his rare tact and insight, he could hardly fail to perceive that this was a document of first-rate importance, yet one of which the evidence could not be satisfactorily reconciled with the comparatively simple hypothesis which he had based on the assumed primacy of the Alexandrine. For his immediate purpose, it was of far less importance that he was partly in error as to his Latin standard. His view on that subject is connected with a curious instance of his boldness in conjectural criticism. Referring to "interpretationes" or versions of the Bible, Augustine once says, "Let the Italian (*Itala*) be preferred to the rest, since it combines greater closeness with clearness" (*De Doctr. Chr.* II. 15). Bentley, with a rashness which even he seldom exceeded, declared that the "Italian version is a mere dream:" *Itala*, in Augustine, should be *illa*. Archbishop Potter's *usitata*, viewed merely as an emendation, was far more intrinsically probable; but Cardinal Wiseman's arguments in his letters (1832–3)—reinforced by Lachmann's illustrations—have placed it beyond reasonable doubt that Augustine really wrote *Itala*. As to his meaning, all that is certain is that he intended to distinguish this "Italian" text from the "African" (*codices Afros*) which he mentions elsewhere. Of a Latin version, or Latin versions, prior to Jerome's—which was a recension, with the aid of Greek MSS., not a new and original version—Bentley

8*

could scarcely know anything. The documents were first
made accessible in Bianchini's *Evangeliarium Quadruplex*
(1749), and the Benedictine Sabatier's *Bibliorum Sacro-
rum Latinae Versiones Antiquae* (1751). It must be remembered, however, that Bentley's aim was to restore the
text as received in the fourth century; he did not profess
to restore the text of an earlier age.

Bentley's edition would have given to the world the
readings of all the older Greek MSS. then known, and an
apparatus, still unequalled in its range of authorities, for
the text of the Latin Vulgate New Testament: but it
would have done more still. Whatever might have been
its defects, it would have represented the earliest attempt
to construct a text of the New Testament directly from
the most ancient documents, without reference to any
printed edition. A century passed before such an attempt
was again made. Bentley's immediate successors in this
field did not work on his distinctive lines. In 1726 Bengel's Greek Testament was almost ready for the press, and
he writes thus: "What principally holds me back is the
delay of Bentley's promised edition. . . . Bentley possesses
invaluable advantages; but he has prepossessions of his
own which may prove very detrimental to the Received
Text:" this "received text" being, in fact, the Syrian text
in its mediæval form. Bengel's text, published at Tübin-
gen in 1734, was not based on Bentley's principles, though
the value of these is incidentally recognised in his discussions. Wetstein's edition of 1751–2 supplied fresh materials; in criticism, however, he represents rather a re-
action from Bentley's view, for his tendency was to find
traces of corruption in any close agreement between the
ancient Greek MSS. and the ancient versions. Gries-
bach prepared the way for a properly critical text by

seeking an historical basis in the genealogy of the documents.

But it was Lachmann, in his small edition of 1831, who first gave a modified fulfilment to Bentley's design, by publishing a text irrespective of the printed tradition, and based wholly on the ancient authorities. Lachmann also applied Bentley's principle of Greek and Latin consent. As Bentley had proposed to use the Vulgate Latin, so Lachmann used what he deemed the best MSS. of the Old Latin—combined with some Latin Fathers and with such Greek MSS. as were manifestly of the same type. Lachmann compared this group of witnesses from the West with the other or "Eastern" Greek authorities; and, where they agreed, he laid stress on that agreement as a security for the genuineness of readings. Bentley had intended to print the Greek text and the Vulgate Latin side by side. Lachmann, in his larger edition (1810 1852), so far executed this plan as to print at the foot of the page a greatly improved Vulgate text, based chiefly on the two oldest MSS. For Lachmann, however, the authority of the Vulgate was only accessory ("*Hieronymo* pro se *auctore non utimur*"), on account of the higher antiquity of the Old Latin. Those who taunted Lachmann with "aping" Bentley ("simia Bentleii") misrepresented both. It is to Lachmann and to Tregelles that we primarily owe the revived knowledge and appreciation in this country of Bentley's labours on the New Testament, to which Tischendorf also accords recognition in his edition of 1859.

Bentley's place in the history of sacred criticism agrees with the general character of his work in other provinces. His ideas were in advance of his age, and also of the means at his disposal for executing them. He gave an

initial impulse, of which the effect could not be destroyed
by the limitation or defeat of his personal labours. After
a hundred years of comparative neglect, his conception re-
appeared as an element of acknowledged value in the
methods of riper research. The edition of the New Testament published last year (1881) by Dr. Westcott and
Dr. Hort represents a stage of criticism which necessarily
lay beyond Bentley's horizon. Yet it is the maturest em-
bodiment of principles which had in him their earliest exponent; and those very delays which closed over his great
design may in part be regarded as attesting his growing
perception of the rule on which the Cambridge Editors so
justly lay stress: "Knowledge of documents should pre-
cede final judgment upon readings."

CHAPTER XI.

As a writer of English, Bentley is represented by the Dissertation on Phalaris, the Boyle Lectures, the Remarks on a Discourse of Free-thinking, sermons, and letters. These fall mainly within the period from 1690 to 1730. During the earlier half of Bentley's life the canon of polite prose was Dryden or Temple; during the latter half it was Addison. Bentley's English is stamped, as we shall see, with the mind of his age, but has been very little influenced by any phase of its manner. His style is thoroughly individual; it is, in fact, the man. The most striking trait is the nervous, homely English. "Commend me to the man that with a thick hide and solid forehead can stand bluff against plain matter of fact." "If the very first Epistle, of nine lines only, has taken me up four pages in scouring, what a sweet piece of work should I have of it to cleanse all the rest for them!" "Alas, poor Sophist! 'twas ill luck he took none of the money, to fee his advocates lustily; for this is like to be a hard brush." The "polite" writers after the Restoration had discarded such English as vulgar; and we have seen that Boyle's Oxford friends complained of Bentley's "descending to low and mean ways of speech." But, if we allow for the special influence of scriptural language on the *Pilgrim's Progress*, Bentley drew from the same well as John Bunyan, who died when Bentley was sixteen. Yet Bentley's simple English is racy in a way peculiar to him. It has the tone of a strong mind which goes straight to the truth; it is pointed with the sarcasm of one whose own knowledge is thorough and exact, but who is accustomed to find imposture wrapped up in fine or vague words, and takes an ironical delight in using the very homeliest images and phrases which accurately fit the matter in hand. No one has excelled Bentley in the power of making a pretentious fallacy absurd by the mere force of translation into simple terms; no writer of English has shown greater skill in touching the hidden springs of its native humour.

Here Bentley is the exponent, in his own way, of a spirit which animated the age of Addison and Pope—the assertion of clear common-sense—the desire, as Mr. Leslie Stephen says, "to expel the mystery which had served as a cloak for charlatans." Bentley's English style reflects, however, another side on which he was not in sympathy with the tendencies of contemporary literature. A scholar of profound learning and original vigour had things to say which could not always be said with the sparkling ease of coffee-house conversation. Bentley's colloquialism is that of strenuous argument, not that of polished small talk. As an outward symbol of his separateness from the "wits," we may observe his use of the Latin element in English. The sermons of Jeremy Taylor, whose life closed soon after Bentley's began, abound in portentous Latin words—*longanimity, recidivation, coadunation*. Bentley has nothing like these; yet the Boyle party, who charged his style with vulgarity, charged it also with pedantry.

He answers this in the Dissertation on Phalaris. "If such a general censure had been always fastened upon those that enrich our language from the Latin and Greek stores, what a fine condition had our language been in! 'Tis well known, it has scarce any words, beside monosyllables, of its native growth; and were all the rest imported and introduced by *pedants?* . . . The words in my book, which he excepts against, are *commentitious, repudiate, concede, aliene, vernacular, timid, negoce, putid,* and *idiom;* every one of which were in print, before I used them; and most of them, before I was born." We note in passing that all but three of this list—*commentitious, putid, negoce*—have lived; and we remember De Quincey's story about *negoce* —that when he was a boy at school (about the year 1798) the use of this word by the master suggested to him that *otium cum dignitate* might be rendered "oce in combination with dignity" which made him laugh aloud, and thereby forfeit all "oce" for three days. Then Bentley remarks that the "Examiner's" illustrious relative, Robert Boyle, had used *ignore* and *recognosce*—"which nobody has yet thought fit to follow him in." It is curious to find De Quincey saying, in 1830, that *ignore* is Irish, and obsolete in England "except in the use of grand juries;" and even in 1857, it seems, some purists demurred to it. "I would rather use, not my own words only, but even these too"—Bentley concludes—"than that single word of the Examiner's, *cotemporary,* which is a downright barbarism. For the Latins never use *co* for *con,* except before a vowel, as *coequal, coeternal;* but, before a consonant, they either retain the N, as *contemporary, constitution;* or melt it into another letter, as *collection, comprehension.* So that the Examiner's *cotemporary* is a word of his *coposition,* for which the learned world will *cogratulate* him."

Bentley's view as to the probable future of the English language appears from another place in the Dissertation. "The great alterations it has undergone in the two last centuries [1500–1700] are principally owing to that vast stock of Latin words which we have transplanted into our own soil: which being now in a manner exhausted, one may easily presage that it will not have such changes in the two next centuries. Nay, it were no difficult contrivance, if the public had any regard to it, to make the English tongue immutable, unless hereafter some foreign nation shall invade and overrun us." This is in seeming contrast with Bentley's own description of language as an organism liable to continual change, "like the perspiring bodies of living creatures in perpetual motion and alteration." But the inconsistency, I think, is only apparent. He refers to the English vocabulary as a whole. By "immutable" he does not mean to exclude the action of time on details of form or usage, but rather points to such a standard as the French Academy sought to fix for the French language. Since the end of the seventeenth century, the ordinary English vocabulary has lost some foreign words, and acquired others; on the whole, the foreign element has probably not gained ground. Here is a rough test. Mr. Marsh has estimated the percentage of English to non-English words in several English classics. Swift's is about 70 (in one essay, only 68); Gibbon's, 70; Johnson's, 72; Macaulay's, 75. Bentley's own average would, I think, be nearly, if not quite, as high as Macaulay's, and for a like reason; his literary diction was comparatively close to the living speech of educated men in his day. This, indeed, is a marked feature of all Bentley's work, whatever the subject or form may be; the author's personality is so vividly present in it that it is less like writing than speaking.

As in Shakspeare, we meet with those faults of grammar which people were apt to make in talking, or which had even come to be thought idiomatic, through the habit of the ear. Bentley can say, "neither of these two improvements *are* registered"—"*those* sort of requests"—"I'll dispute with nobody about *nothing*" (meaning, "about anything")—"no goat had been there *neither*." This sympathy with living speech, and comparative negligence of rigid syntax, may help us to see how Bentley's genius was in accord with Greek, the voice of life, rather than with Latin, the expression of law. The scholarly trait of Bentley's style is not precise composition, but propriety in the use of words, whether of English or of Latin growth. Some of these Latinisms, though etymologically right, seem odd now : "an acuteness *familiar* to him," *i. e.*, peculiarly his own : "*excision*" for "utter destruction :" "a plain and *punctual* testimony" *i. e.*, just to the point. Yet, on the whole, Bentley's vocabulary contains a decidedly larger proportion of pure English than was then usual in the higher literature. No one is less pedantic. At his best he is, in his own way, matchless : at his worst, he is sometimes rough or clumsy ; but he is never weak, and never anything else than natural. His style in hand-to-hand critical combat—as in the Phalaris Dissertation—is that by which he is best known. I may here give a short specimen of a different manner, from a Sermon which he preached at St. James's in 1717. He is speaking on the words, "none of us liveth to himself" (Romans xiv. 7) :

"Without society and government, man would be found in a worse condition than the very beasts of the field. That divine ray of reason, which is his privilege above the brutes, would only serve in that case to make him more sensible of his wants, and more uneasy and melancholic under them. Now, if society and mutual friendship be so essential and necessary to the happiness of mankind, 'tis a clear consequence, that all such obligations as are necessary to maintain society and friendship are incumbent on every man. No one, therefore, that lives in society, and expects his share in the benefits of it, can be said to live to himself.

"No, he lives to his prince and his country; he lives to his parents and his family; he lives to his friends and to all under his trust; he lives even to foreigners, under the mutual sanctions and stipulations of alliance and commerce; nay, he lives to the whole race of mankind: whatsoever has the character of man, and wears the same image of God that he does, is truly his brother, and, on account of that natural consanguinity, has a just claim to his kindness and benevolence. . . . The nearer one can arrive to this universal charity, this benevolence to all human race, the more he has of the divine character imprinted on his soul; for *God is love*, says the apostle; he delights in the happiness of all his creatures. To this public principle we owe our thanks for the inventors of sciences and arts; for the founders of kingdoms, and first institutors of laws; for the heroes that hazard or abandon their own lives for the dearer love of their country; for the statesmen that generously sacrifice their private profit and ease to establish the public peace and prosperity for ages to come.

"And if nature's still voice be listened to, this is really not only the noblest, but the pleasantest employment. For though gratitude, and a due acknowledgment and return of kindness received, is a desirable good, and implanted in our nature by God himself, as a spur to mutual beneficence, yet, in the whole, 'tis certainly much more pleasant to love than to be beloved again. For the sweetness and felicity of life consists in duly exerting and employing those sociable passions of the soul, those natural inclinations to charity and compassion. And he that has given his mind a contrary turn and bias, that has made it the seat of selfishness and of unconcernment for all about him, has deprived himself of the greatest comfort and relish of life. Whilst he foolishly designs to live to himself alone, he loses that very thing which makes life itself desirable. So that, in a word, if we are created by our Maker to enjoy happiness and contentment in our being; if we are born for society, and friendship, and mutual assistance; if we are designed to live as men, and not as wild beasts of the desert; we must truly say, in the words of our text, that none of us *liveth to himself*."

It will be noticed that in the above extract there are no sentences of unwieldy length, no involved constructions, such as usually encumbered the more elaborate prose of the seventeenth century. Comparatively short sentences, and lucid structure, are general marks of Bentley's English; and here, again, he reflects the desire of his age for *clearness*. It has been said that the special work of the eighteenth century was to form prose style. Bentley has his peculiar place among its earlier masters.

Mention is due to the only English verses which he is known to have written after boyhood. When Johnson recited them, Adam Smith remarked that they were "very well; very well." "Yes, they *are* very well, sir," said Johnson; "but you may observe in what manner they are well. They are the forcible verses of a man of strong mind, but not accustomed to write verse; for there is some uncouthness in the expression." A Trinity undergraduate had written a graceful imitation of Horace's Ode, *Angustam amice pauperiem pati* (III. ii.); with which Bentley was so much pleased that he straightway composed a parody on it. The gist of the young man's piece is that an exemplary student is secure of applause and happiness; Bentley sings that he is pretty sure to be attacked, and very likely to be shelved. The choice of typical men is interesting; Newton, and the geologist, John Woodward, for science; Selden, for erudition; for theological controversy, Whiston, whom the University had expelled on account of his Arianism. (The following is Monk's version: Boswell's differs in a few points, mostly for the worse; but in v. 11 rightly gives "days and nights" for "day and night.")

"Who strives to mount Parnassus' hill,
   And thence poetic laurels bring,
Must first acquire due force and skill,
   Must fly with swan's or eagle's wing.

"Who Nature's treasures would explore,
   Her mysteries and arcana know,
Must high, as lofty NEWTON, soar,
   Must stoop, as delving WOODWARD, low.

"Who studies ancient laws and rites,
   Tongues, arts, and arms, all history,
Must drudge, like SELDEN, days and nights,
   And in the endless labour die.

"Who travels* in religious jarrs,   * ? *travails.*
   Truth mix'd with error, shade with rays,
Like WHISTON, wanting pyx and stars,
   In ocean wide or sinks or strays.

"But grant our hero's hope, long toil
   And comprehensive genius crown,
All sciences, all arts his spoil,
   Yet what reward, or what renown?

"ENVY, innate in vulgar souls,
   Envy steps in and stops his rise;
Envy with poison'd tarnish fouls
   His lustre, and his worth decries.

"He lives inglorious or in want,
   To college and old books confin'd;
Instead of learn'd, he's call'd pedànt;
   Dunces advanc'd, he's left behind:
Yet left content, a genuine stoic he,
Great without patron, rich without South-sea."

The third line from the end is significant. He had
been mentioned for a bishopric once or twice, but passed

over. In 1709, when Chichester was vacant, Baron Spanheim and the Earl of Pembroke (then Lord High Admi-
ral) had vainly used their interest for Bentley. We have
seen that in 1724—about two years after these verses were
written—he declined the see of Bristol.

Now we must consider Bentley's criticisms on *Paradise
Lost.* In 1725 an edition of that poem had appeared
with a Life of Milton by Elijah Fenton (1683–1730), who
helped Pope in translating the *Odyssey.* Fenton incidentally suggested some corrections of words which, he
thought, might have taken the place of other words similar in sound. This seems to have put Bentley on his
mettle: at any rate, he is said to have meditated notes in
1726. His edition of *Paradise Lost* appeared in 1732,
and is said to have been immediately due to a wish expressed by Queen Caroline "that the great critic should
exercise his talents upon an edition" of Milton, "and thus
gratify those readers who could not enjoy his celebrated
lucubrations on classical writers." It may safely be assumed, however, that the royal lady did not contemplate
any such work as our Aristarchus produced. Probably
she thought that the learning, especially classical learning,
which enters so largely into Milton's epic would afford a
good field for illustrative commentary to a classical scholar.

" 'Tis but common justice"—Bentley's preface begins
—"to let the purchaser know what he is to expect in this
new edition of *Paradise Lost.* Our celebrated Author,
when he compos'd this poem, being obnoxious to the Government, poor, friendless, and, what is worst of all, blind
with a *gutta serena,* could only dictate his verses to be
writ by another." The amanuensis made numerous mistakes in spelling and pointing; Bentley says that he has
tacitly corrected these merely clerical errors. But there

was a more serious offender than the amanuensis; namely, the *editor*. This person owes his existence to Bentley's vigorous imagination. "The friend or acquaintance, whoever he was, to whom Milton committed his copy and the overseeing of the press, did so vilely execute that trust, that *Paradise* under his ignorance and audaciousness may be said to be *twice lost*." This editor is responsible for many careless changes of word or phrase; for instance:

> "on the secret top
> Of Horeb or of Sinai—"

"secret" is this editor's blunder for "sacred." Bentley gives 48 examples of such culpable carelessness. But even that is not the worst. "This suppos'd Friend (call'd in these Notes the Editor), knowing Milton's bad circumstances"—the evil days and evil tongues—profited by them to perpetrate a deliberate fraud of the most heartless kind. Having a turn for verse-writing, he actually interpolated many lines of his own; Bentley gives 66 of them as examples. They can always be "detected by their own silliness and unfitness." So much for the half-educated amanuensis and the wholly depraved editor. But Milton himself has made some "slips and inadvertencies too;" there are "some inconsistences [*sic*] in the system and plan of his poem, for want of his revisal of the whole before its publication." Sixteen examples are then given. These are beyond merely verbal emendation. They require "a change both of words and sense." Bentley lays stress on the fact that he merely suggests remedies for the errors due to Milton himself, but does not "obtrude" them; adding, "it is hoped, even these will not be found absurd, or disagreeing from the Miltonian character;" and he quotes from Virgil: "I, too, have written verses: me

also the shepherds call a singer; but I will not lightly believe them." This is perhaps the only thing in the preface that distinctly suggests senility; it afterwards gave
rise to this doggrel:

> "How could vile sycophants contrive
>   A lie so gross to raise,
> Which even Bentley can't believe,
>   Though spoke in his own praise?"

The preface concludes with a glowing tribute to Milton's
great poem. Labouring under all this "miserable de-
formity by the press," it could still charm, like "Terence's
beautiful Virgin, who, in spite of neglect, sorrow, and beg-
garly habit, did yet appear so very amiable." There is
some real pathos in the following passage—remarkable
as the only one (so far as I know) in Bentley's writings
where he alludes to the long troubles of his College life as
causes of *pain*, and not merely of interruption:

> "But I wonder not so much at the poem itself, though worthy of all
> wonder; as that the author could so abstract his thoughts from his
> own troubles, as to be able to make it; that confin'd in a narrow
> and to him a dark chamber, surrounded with cares and fears, he
> could spatiate at large through the compass of the whole universe,
> and through all heaven beyond it; could survey all periods of time,
> from before the creation to the consummation of all things. This
> theory [*i.e.*, contemplation], no doubt, was a great solace to him in
> his affliction; but it shows in him a greater strength of spirit, that
> made him capable of such a solace. And it would almost seem to
> me to be peculiar to him; had not experience by others taught me,
> that there is that power in the human mind, supported with inno-
> cence and *conscia virtus;* that can make it quite shake off all out-
> ward uneasinesses, and involve itself secure and pleas'd in its own
> integrity and entertainment."

Bentley appears to have fully anticipated the strong
prejudice which his recension of Milton would have to

meet. Forty years ago, he says, "it would have been
prudence to have suppress'd" it, "for fear of injuring
one's rising fortune." But now seventy years admonished him to pay his critical debts, regardless of worldly loss
or gain. "I made the Notes extempore, and put them
to the press as soon as made; without any apprehension
of growing leaner by censures or plumper by commenda-
tions." So ends the preface.

Bentley's work on Milton is of a kind which can be
fairly estimated by a few specimens, for its essential character is the same throughout. We need not dwell on
those "inconsistencies in the plan and system of the
poem" which Bentley ascribes to Milton himself. Some
of these are real, others vanish before a closer examination; but none of those which really exist can be removed
without rewriting the passages affected. Bentley admits
this; and to criticise his changes would be merely to compare the respective merits of Milton and Bentley as poets.
Nor, again, need we concern ourselves with those alleged
faults of the amanuensis in spelling and pointing which
are tacitly corrected. The proper test of Bentley's work,
as a critical recension of *Paradise Lost*, is his treatment
of those blemishes which he imputes to the supposed
"editor." These are of two kinds—wilful interpolations
and inadvertent changes. An example of alleged interpolation is afforded by the following passage (*Par. Lost*, I.
338–355), where the fallen angels are assembling at the
summons of their leader:

> "As when the potent rod
> Of Amram's son, in Egypt's evil day,
> Waved round the coast, up-called a pitchy cloud
> Of locusts, warping on the eastern wind,
> That o'er the realm of impious Pharaoh hung
> Like Night, and darkened all the land of Nile;

> So numberless were those bad Angels seen
> Hovering on wing under the cope of Hell,
> 'Twixt upper, nether, and surrounding fires;
> Till, as a signal given, the uplifted spear
> Of their great Sultan waving to direct
> Their course, in even balance down they light
> On the firm brimstone, and fill all the plain:
> *A multitude like which the populous North*
> *Poured never from her frozen loins to pass*
> *Rhene or the Danaw, when her barbarous sons*
> *Came like a deluge on the South, and spread*
> *Beneath Gibraltar to the Libyan sands.*"

The last five lines are rejected by Bentley as due to the fraudulent editor.   Here is his note:

"After he [Milton] had compared the Devils for number to the cloud of locusts that darken'd all Egypt, as before to the leaves that cover the ground in autumn [v. 302, 'Thick as autumnal leaves that strew the brooks In Vallombrosa'], 'tis both to clog and to lessen the thought, to mention here the Northern Excursions, when all human race would be too few.   Besides the diction is faulty; *frozen loins* are improper for *populousness;* Gibraltar is a new name, since those inroads were made; and to spread from thence to the Libyan sands, is to spread over the surface of the sea."

It would be idle to multiply instances of "interpolation:" this is a fair average sample.   I will now illustrate the other class of "editorial" misdeeds—careless alterations.   Book VI. 509:

> "Up they turned
> Wide the celestial soil, and saw beneath
> The originals of Nature in their crude
> Conception; sulphurous and nitrous foam
> *They found, they mingled, and, with subtle art*
> Concocted and adusted, they reduced
> To blackest grain, and into store conveyed."

Bentley annotates:

9

"It must be very subtle Art, even in Devils themselves, to adust brimstone and saltpetre.   But then he mentions only these two materials, which without *charcoal* can never make gunpowder."

Here, then, is the last part of the passage, rescued from the editor, and restored to Milton:

> "Sulphurous and nitrous foam
> *They pound, they mingle, and with sooty chark*
> Concocted and adusted, they *reduce*
> To blackest grain, and into store *convey*."

Let us take next the last lines of the poem (XII. 641 f.):

> "They, looking back, all the eastern side beheld
> Of Paradise, so late their happy seat,
> Waved over by that flaming brand; the gate
> With dreadful faces thronged and fiery arms.
> Some natural tears they dropped, but wiped them soon;
> The world was all before them, where to choose
> Their place of rest, and Providence their guide.
> *They, hand in hand, with wandering steps and slow,*
> *Through Eden took their solitary way.*"

Addison had remarked that the poem would close better if the last two lines were absent.   Bentley—without naming Addison, to whom he alludes as "an ingenious and celebrated writer"—deprecates their omission.   "Without them Adam and Eve would be left in the Territory and Suburbane of Paradise, in the very view of the *dreadful faces.*"   At the same time Bentley holds that the two lines have been gravely corrupted by the editor.   These are his grounds:

"Milton tells us before, that Adam, upon hearing Michael's predictions, was even surcharg'd with joy (XII. 372); was replete with joy and wonder (468); was in doubt, whether he should repent of, or rejoice in, his fall (475); was in great peace of thought (558); and Eve herself was *not sad*, but full of *consolation* (620).   Why then does this distich dismiss our first parents in anguish, and the reader in melancholy? And how can the expression be justified, 'with wand'ring steps and slow?' Why *wan'dring?* Erratic steps? Very improper: when in the line before, they were guided by Providence. And why *slow?* when even Eve profess'd her readiness and alacrity for the journey (614): '*But now lead on; In me is no delay.*' And why 'their solitary way?' All words to represent a sorrowful parting? when even their former walks in Paradise were as solitary as their way now: there being nobody besides them two, both here and there. Shall I therefore, after so many prior presumptions, presume at last to offer a distich, as close as may be to the author's words, and entirely agreeable to his scheme?

> ' *Then* hand in hand *with social steps their way*
> Through Eden took, *with heav'nly comfort cheer'd.*' "

The total number of emendations proposed by Bentley in *Paradise Lost* rather exceeds 800. Not a word of the received text is altered in his edition; but the parts believed to be corrupt are printed in italics, with the proposed remedy in the margin. Most of the new readings aim at stricter propriety in the use of language, better logic, or clearer syntax—briefly, at " correctness." It is a significant fact that Pope liked many of them, and wrote "*pulchre*," " *bene*," " *recte* " opposite them in his copy of Bentley's edition—in spite of that line in the *Dunciad* which describes our critic as " having humbled Milton's strains." But even where we concede that the new reading is what Milton ought to have given, we can nearly always feel morally certain that he did not give it. I have found only one instance which strikes me as an exception. It is in that passage of Book VI. (332) which describes Satan wounded by the sword of the archangel Michael:

> " From the gash
> A stream of nectarous humour issuing flowed
> Sanguine, such as celestial Spirits may bleed."

"Nectar" is the wine of the gods; Homer has another
name for the etherial juice which flows in their veins.
Thus when Diomedes wounds the goddess Aphrodite:
"*The immortal blood of the goddess flowed forth, even
ichor, such as flows in the veins of blessed gods* (Iliad, v.
389). For "nectarous" Bentley proposed "ichorous."
The form of Milton's verse—"such as celestial Spirits
may bleed"—indicates that he was thinking of the Iliad,
and no poet was less likely than Milton to confuse "nectar" with "ichor." Bentley's correction, if not true, deserves to be so.

Johnson has characterised Bentley's hypothesis of the
"editor" in well-known terms—"a supposition rash and
groundless, if he thought it true; and vile and pernicious,
if, as is said, he in private allowed it to be false." Bentley cannot be impaled on the second horn of the dilemma.
No one who has read his preface, or, who understands the
bent of his mind, will entertain the idea that he wished
to impose on his readers by a fiction which he himself did
not believe. Monk has another explanation. "The ideal
agency of the reviser of *Paradise Lost* was only a device
to take off the odium of perpetually condemning and altering the words of the great poet. . . . At the same time,
he was neither deceived himself, nor intended to deceive
others." But Monk has not observed that a passage in
Bentley's preface expressly excludes this plausible view.
"If any one" (says Bentley) "fancy this *Persona* of an
editor to be a mere Fantom, a Fiction, an Artifice to skreen
Milton himself; let him consider these four and sole changes
made in the second edition: i. 505, v. 638, xi. 485, 551.
. . . If the Editor durst insert his forgeries, even in the
second edition, when the Poem and its Author had slowly
grown to a vast reputation; what durst he not do in the

first, under the poet's poverty, infamy, and an universal
odium from the royal and triumphant party ?" The *Paradise Regained* and the *Samson Agonistes* are uncor-
rupted, Bentley adds, because Milton had then dismissed
this editor.

There can be no doubt, I think, that Bentley's theory
of the depraved editor was broached in perfect good faith.
True, he supposes this editor to have taken fewer liberties
with Book xii.—an assumption which suited his desire to
publish before Parliament met. But that is only an instance of a man bringing himself to believe just what he
wishes to believe. How he could believe it, is another
question. If he had consulted the Life of Milton by the
poet's nephew, Edward Phillips (1694), he would have
found some adverse testimony. *Paradise Lost* was originally written down in small groups of some ten to thirty
verses by any hand that happened to be near Milton at
the time. But, when it was complete, Phillips helped his
uncle in carefully revising it, with minute attention to
those matters of spelling and pointing in which the amanuensis might have failed. The first edition (1667), so far
from being "miserably deformed by the press," was remarkably accurate. As Mr. Masson says, "very great care
must have been bestowed on the revising of the proofs,
either by Milton himself, or by some competent person
who had undertaken to see the book through the press
for him. It seems likely that Milton himself caused page
after page to be read over slowly to him, and occasionally
even the words to be spelt out." Bentley insists that the
changes in the second edition of 1674 were due to the
editor. Phillips says of this second edition: "amended,
enlarg'd, and differently dispos'd as to the number of
books" [xii. instead of x., books vii. and x. being now

divided] " by his own hand, that is by his own appointment." But the habit of mind which Bentley had formed
by free conjectural criticism was such as to pass lightly
over any such difficulties, even if he had clearly realised
them. He felt confident in his own power of improving
Milton's text; and he was eager to exercise it. The fact
of Milton's blindness suggested a view of the text which
he adopted; not, assuredly, without believing it; but with
a belief rendered more easy by his wish.

Bentley's *Paradise Lost* raises an obvious question.
We know that his emendations of Milton are nearly all
bad. The general style of argument which he applies to
Milton is the same which he applies to the classical authors. Are his emendations of these also bad? I should
answer: Many of his critical emendations, especially Latin, are bad; but many of them are good in a way and in
a degree for which *Paradise Lost* afforded no scope. It
is a rule applicable to most of Bentley's corrections, that
their merit varies inversely with the soundness of the text.
Where the text seemed altogether hopeless, he was at his
best; where it was corrupted, but not deeply, he was usually good, though often not convincing; where it was true,
yet difficult, through some trick (faulty in itself, perhaps)
of individual thought or style, he was apt to meddle over-
much. It was his forte to make rough places smooth; his
foible, to make smooth places rough. If *Paradise Lost*
had come to Bentley as a manuscript, largely defaced by
grave blunders and deeply-seated corruptions, his restoration of it would probably have deserved applause. The
fact that his edition was regarded as a proof of dotage,
shows how erroneously his contemporaries had conceived
the qualities of his previous work. Bentley's mind was
logical, positive, acute; wonderfully acute, where intellect-

ual problems were not complicated with moral sympathies. Sending flashes of piercing insight over a wide and then dim field, he made discoveries; among other things, he found probable or certain answers to many verbal riddles. His "faculty of divination" was to himself a special source of joy and pride; nor unnaturally, when we recall its most brilliant feats. But verbal emendation was only one phase of his work; and, just because it was with him a mental indulgence, almost a passion, we must guard against assuming that the *average* success with which he applied it is the chief criterion of his power.

The faults of Bentley's *Paradise Lost* are, in kind, the faults of his Horace, but are more evident to an English reader, and are worse in degree, since the English text, unlike the Latin, affords no real ground for suspicion. The intellectual acuteness which marks the Horace is present also in the notes on *Paradise Lost*, but seldom wins admiration, more often appears ridiculous, because the English reader can usually see that it is grotesquely misplaced. A great and characteristic merit of Bentley's classical work, its instructiveness to students of a foreign language and literature, is necessarily absent here. And the book was got ready for the press with extreme haste. Still, the editor of *Paradise Lost* is not the Horatian editor gone mad. He is merely the Horatian editor showing increased rashness in a still more unfavourable field, where failure was at once so gratuitous and so conspicuous as to look like self-caricature, whilst there was no proper scope for the distinctive qualities of his genius. As to poetical taste, we may at least make some allowance for the standards of the "correct" period: let us think of Johnson's remarks on Milton's versification, and remember that some of Bentley's improvements on Milton were privately admired by Pope.

CHAPTER XII.

AT the age of thirty-eight, when explaining his delay to answer Charles Boyle, Bentley spoke of his own "natural aversion to all quarrels and broils." This has often, perhaps, been read with a smile by those who thought of his later feuds. I believe that it was quite true. Bentley was a born student. He was not, by innate impulse, a writer, still less an aspirant to prizes of the kind for which men chiefly wrangle. But his self-confidence had been exalted by the number of instances in which he had been able to explode fallacies, or to detect errors which had escaped the greatest of previous scholars. He became a dogmatic believer in the truth of his own instinctive perceptions. At last, opposition to his decrees struck him as a proof of deficient capacity, or else of moral obliquity. This habit of mind insensibly extended itself from verbal criticism into other fields of judgment. He grew less and less fit to deal with men on a basis of equal rights, because he too often carried into official or social intercourse the temper formed in his library by intellectual despotism over the blunders of the absent or the dead. He was rather too apt to treat those who differed from him as if they were various readings that had cropped up from "scrub manuscripts," or "scoundrel copies," as he has it in his reply to

Middleton. He liked to efface such persons as he would expunge false concords, or to correct them as he would remedy flagrant instances of hiatus. This was what made him so specially unfit for the peaceable administration of a College. It was hard for him to be *primus inter pares*—first among peers, but harder still to be *primus intra parietes*—to live within the same walls with those peers. The frequent personal association which the circumstances of his office involved was precisely calculated to show him constantly on his worst side. He would probably have made a better bishop—though not, perhaps, a very good one—just because his contact would have been less close and continual with those over whom he was placed. Bentley had many of the qualities of a beneficent ruler, but hardly of a constitutional ruler. If he had been the sole heir of Peisistratus, he would have bestowed the best gifts of paternal government on those Athenian blacksmiths to whom he compared Joshua Barnes, and no swords would have been wreathed with myrtle in honour of a tyrannicide.

This warm-hearted, imperious man, with affections the stronger because they were not diffuse, was seen to the greatest advantage in family life, either because his monarchy was undisputed, or because there he could reign without governing. His happy marriage brought him four children—Elizabeth and Joanna—a son, William, who died in earliest infancy—and Richard, the youngest, born in 1708, who grew to be an accomplished but eccentric and rather aimless man; enough of a dilettante to win the good graces of Horace Walpole, and too little of a dependent to keep them.

It is pleasant to turn from the College feuds, and to think that within its precincts there was at least such a

9*

refuge from strife as the home in which these children grew up. The habits of the Bentley household were simple, and such as adapted themselves to the life of an indefatigable student. Bentley usually breakfasted alone in his library, and, at least in later years, was often not visible till dinner. When the *Spectator* was coming out, he took great delight in hearing the children read it aloud to him, and—as Joanna told her son—"was so particularly amused by the character of Sir Roger de Coverley, that he took his literary decease most seriously to heart." After evening prayers at ten, the family retired, while Bentley, "habited in his dressing-gown," returned to his books. In 1708 his eyes suffered for a short time from reading at night; but he kept up the habit long afterwards. The celebrated "Proposals for Printing" the Greek Testament were drawn up by candle-light in a single evening. Latterly, he had a few intimate friends at Cambridge—some five or six Fellows of the College, foremost among whom was Richard Walker—and three or four other members of the University; just as in London his intercourse was chiefly with a very small and select group—Newton, Dr. Samuel Clarke, Dr. Mead, and a few more. "His establishment," says his grandson, "was respectable, and his table affluently and hospitably served." "Of his pecuniary affairs he took no account; he had no use for money, and dismissed it entirely from his thoughts." Mrs. Bentley managed everything. Can this be the Bentley, it will be asked, who built the staircase and the hen-house, and who practised extortion on the Doctors of Divinity? The fact seems to be, as Cumberland puts it, that Bentley had no love of money for its own sake. Many instances of his liberality are on record, especially to poor students, or in literary matters. But he had a strong feeling for the dignity of his station, and a frank conviction that the College ought to honour itself by seeing that his surroundings were appropriate; and he had also a Yorkshireman's share of the British dislike to being cheated. Bentley's total income was, for his position, but moderate, and his testamentary provision for his family was sufficiently slender to exempt him from the charge of penurious hoarding.

At one time Mrs. Bentley and the children used to make an annual journey to London, where the Master of Trinity, as Royal Librarian, had official lodgings at Cotton House. Then there was an occasional visit to the Bernards in Huntingdónshire, or to Hampshire, after Elizabeth, the eldest daughter, had married Mr. Humphrey Ridge of that county; and this was as much variety as the wisdom of our ancestors desired. At Cambridge Bentley took scarcely any exercise, except in pacing up and down a terrace-walk by the river, which was made when the Master's garden was laid out in 1717. We hear, however, of his joining a fishing expedition to Over, a place about six miles from Cambridge, though some may doubt whether Bentley had the right temperament for that pursuit. After middle age he was peculiarly liable to severe colds —a result of sedentary life—and was obliged to avoid draughts as much as possible. From 1727 he ceased to preside in the College Hall at festivals; and at about the same time he nominated a deputy at the "acts" in the Divinity School. In 1729 it was complained that for many years he had discontinued his attendance in the College Chapel. One incident has good evidence. On an evening in 1724, just after his degrees had been restored, he went to the Chapel; the door-lock of the Master's stall was so rusty that he could not open it. Here are some contemporary verses preserved by Granger:

> " The virger tugs with fruitless pains ;
>   The rust invincible remains.
>   Who can describe his woful plight,
>   Plac'd thus in view, in fullest light,
>   A spectacle of mirth, expos'd
>   To sneering friends and giggling foes ?
>   Then first, as 'tis from fame receiv'd
>   (But fame can't always be believ'd),
>   A blush, the sign of new-born grace,
>   Gleam'd through the horrors of his face.
>   He held it shameful to retreat,
>   And worse to take the lower seat.
>   The virger soon, with nimble bound,
>   At once vaults o'er the wooden mound,
>   And gives the door a furious knock,
>   Which forc'd the disobedient lock."

After 1734 he practically ceased to attend the meetings
of the Seniority : the last occasion on which he presided
was Nov. 8, 1737. His inability or reluctance to leave his
house is shown in 1739 by a curious fact. A Fellow of
a College had been convicted of atheistical views by a
private letter which another member of the same society
had picked up in the quadrangle—and read. The meeting
of the Vice-chancellor's Court at which sentence was to
be passed was held at Trinity Lodge. Dr. Monk regards
this as a "compliment to the father of the University,"
but there was also a simpler motive. Only eight Heads
of Houses had attended in the Schools; nine were required for a verdict; and, feeling the improbability of
Bentley coming to them, they went to Bentley. On seeing the accused—a puny person—the Master of Trinity
observed, " What ! is that the atheist ? I expected to
have seen a man as big as Burrough the beadle !" Sentence was passed—expulsion from the University.

It seems to have been soon after this, in 1739, that

Bentley had a paralytic stroke—not a severe one, however. He was thenceforth unable to move easily without assistance, but we have his grandson's authority for saying that Bentley "to the last hour of his life possessed his faculties firm and in their fullest vigour." He called himself—Markland says—"an old trunk, which, if you let it alone, will last a long time; but if you jumble it by moving, will soon fall to pieces."

Joanna Bentley, the second daughter, was her father's favourite child—"Jug" was his pet-name for her—and she seems to have inherited much of his vivacity, with rather more of his turn for humorous satire than was at that period thought quite decorous in the gentle sex. Her son seems inclined to apologise for it; and Dr. Monk, too, faintly hints his regret. At the age of eleven she was the "Phœbe" of a Pastoral in the *Spectator*—the "Colin" being John Dyrom, B.A., of Trinity; and, after causing several members of the College to sigh, and a few to sing, Joanna was married, in 1728, to Denison Cumberland, of Trinity—a grandson of the distinguished Bishop of Peterborough. Their son, Richard Cumberland, was a versatile author. Besides novels, comedies, and an epic poem, he wrote the once popular *Observer*, and *Anecdotes of Spanish Painters*. Goldsmith called him "the Terence of England;" Walter Scott commented on his tendency "to reverse the natural and useful practice of courtship, and to throw upon the softer sex the task of wooing;" but Cumberland's name has no record more pleasing than those *Memoirs* to which we chiefly owe our knowledge of Bentley's old age.

It was early in 1740 that death parted the old man from the companion who had shared so many years of storm or sunshine beyond the doors, but always of happi-

ness within them. Richard Cumberland was eight years
old when Mrs. Bentley died. " I have a perfect recollec-
tion of the person of my grandmother, and a full impression of her manners and habits, which, though in some
degree tinctured with hereditary reserve and the primitive cast of character, were entirely free from the hyp-
ocritical cant and affected sanctity of the Oliverians."
(Her family, the Bernards, were related to the Cromwells.)
A most favourable impression is given by a letter—one of
those printed by Dr. Luard at the end of Rud's *Diary*—
in which she discusses the prospect (in 1732) of the College case being decided against Bentley. Her life had
been gentle, kindly, and unselfish ; her last words, which
her daughter Joanna heard, were—" It is all bright, it is
all glorious." Dreary indeed must have been Bentley's
solitude now, but for his daughters. Elizabeth had returned to her father's house after the death of her hus-
band, Mr. Ridge ; and henceforth Mrs. Cumberland was
much at Trinity Lodge, with her two children—Richard,
and a girl somewhat older. And now we get the best
possible testimony to the lovable elements in Bentley's
nature—the testimony of children. " He was the un-
wearied patron and promoter of all our childish sports. . . .
I have broken in upon him many a time " (says Cumberland) "in his hours of study, when he would put his book
aside, ring his hand-bell for his servant, and be led to his
shelves to take down a picture-book for my amusement. I
do not say that his good-nature always gained its object,
as the pictures which his books generally supplied me
with were anatomical drawings of dissected bodies, . . .
but he had nothing better to produce." " Once, and only
once, I recollect his giving me a gentle rebuke for making
a most outrageous noise in the room over his library, and

disturbing him in his studies; I had no apprehension of anger from him, and confidently answered that I could not help it, as I had been at battledore and shuttlecock with Master Gooch, the Bishop of Ely's son." (This was the Dr. Gooch who, as Vice-chancellor, had suspended Bentley's degrees.) "And I have been at this sport with his father," he replied; "but thine has been the more amusing game; so there's no harm done." The boy's holidays from his school at Bury St. Edmund's were now often spent at Trinity Lodge, and in the bright memories which they left with him his grandfather was the central figure. "I was admitted to dine at his table, had my seat next to his chair, served him in many little offices." Bentley saw what pleasure these gave the boy, and invented occasions to employ him.

Bentley's "ordinary style of conversation was naturally lofty"—his grandson says. He also used *thou* and *thee* more than was usually considered polite, and this gave his talk a somewhat dictatorial tone. "But the native candour and inherent tenderness of his heart could not long be veiled from observation, for his feelings and affections were at once too impulsive to be long repressed, and he too careless of concealment to attempt at qualifying them." Instances of his good-nature are quoted which are highly characteristic in other ways too. At that time the Master and Seniors examined candidates for Fellowships orally as well as on paper. If Bentley saw that a candidate was nervous, he "was never known to press him," says Cumberland; rather he "would take all the pains of expounding on himself"—and credit the embarrassed youth with the answer. Once a burglar who had stolen some of Bentley's plate was caught "with the very articles upon him," and "Commissary Greaves" was for sending him to gaol. Bentley interposed. "Why tell the man he is a thief? He knows that well enough, without thy information, Greaves.—Hark ye, fellow, thou see'st the trade which thou hast taken up is an unprofitable trade; therefore get thee gone, lay aside an occupation by which thou can'st gain nothing but a halter, and follow that by which thou may'st earn an honest livelihood." Everybody remonstrated, but the burglar was set at large. This was a thoroughly Bentleian way of showing how the quality of mercy can bless him that gives and him that takes. He never bestowed a thought on the principle; he was preoccupied by his own acute and confident perception that *this* man would not steal again; and he disposed of Commissary Greaves as if he had been a mere gloss, a redundant phrase due to interpolation.

Next to the Vice-master, Dr. Walker—to whom in 1739 the duties of Master were virtually transferred—Bentley's most frequent visitors were a few scholars—such as Jeremiah Markland, an ingenious critic, with a real feeling for language; Walter Taylor, the Regius Professor of Greek; John Taylor, the well-known editor of Lysias and Demosthenes; and the two nephews, Thomas and Richard Bentley. At seventy, he learned to smoke; and he is believed to have liked port, but to have said of claret that "it would be port if it could." He would sometimes speak of his early labours and aims, but the literary subject uppermost in his mind seems to have been his Homer. One evening, when Richard Cumberland was at the Lodge in his holidays, his school-master, Arthur Kinsman, called with Dr. Walker. Kinsman "began to open his school-books upon Bentley, and had drawn him into Homer; Greek now rolled in torrents from the lips of Bentley, . . . in a strain delectable, indeed, to the ear, but not very edifying to poor little me and the ladies."

In March, 1742—about four months before Bentley's death—the fourth book of the *Dunciad* came out, with Pope's highly-wrought but curiously empty satire on the greatest scholar then living in England or in Europe. Bentley heads an academic throng who offer homage at the throne of Dulness:

> "Before them march'd that awful Aristarch,
>   Plow'd was his front with many a deep remark:
>   His hat, which never vail'd to human pride,
>   Walker with rev'rence took, and laid aside."

Then Bentley introduces himself to the goddess as

> "Thy mighty scholiast, whose unwearied pains
>   Made Horace dull, and humbled Milton's strains."

The final touch—" Walker, our hat! —nor more he deign'd to say "—was taken from a story current then. Philip Miller, the botanist, had called on Bentley at Trinity Lodge, and after dinner plied him with classical questions, until Bentley, having exhausted such mild hints as "Drink your wine, sir!" exclaimed, "Walker! my hat"— and left the room. Cumberland remembers the large, broad-brimmed hat hanging on a peg at the back of Bentley's arm-chair, who sometimes wore it in his study to shade his eyes; and after his death it could be seen in the College-rooms of the friend with whose name Pope has linked it.

Pope had opened fire on Bentley long before this. The first edition of the *Dunciad* (1728) had the line—"*Bentley* his mouth with classic flatt'ry opes"—but in the edition of 1729 "Bentley" was changed to *Welsted ;* and when—after Bentley's death—his name was once more placed there, it was explained as referring to *Thomas* Bentley, the nephew. Then, in the "Epistle to Arbuthnot" (1735), Pope coupled Bentley with the Shakspearian critic Theobald—"Tibbalds" rhyming to "ribalds;" and in the Epistle imitating that of Horace to Augustus (1737), after criticising Milton, adds:

> "Not that I'd lop the beauties from his book,
> Like slashing Bentley with his desp'rate hook."

Some indignant protest from Thomas Bentley seems to have roused Pope's ire to the more elaborate attack in the fourth book of the *Dunciad*. Why did Pope dislike Bentley? "I talked against his Homer"—this was Bentley's own account of it—"and the portentous cub never forgives." It is more likely that some remarks had been repeated to Pope, than that Bentley should have said to the poet at Bishop Atterbury's table, "A pretty poem, Mr. Pope, but you must not call it Homer." This was gossip dramatising the cause of the grudge. Then Pope's friendship with Atterbury and Swift would lead him to take the Boyle view of the Phalaris affair. And Warburton, Pope's chief ally of the *Dunciad* period, felt towards Bentley that peculiar form of jealous antipathy with which an inaccurate writer on scholarly subjects will sometimes regard scholars. After Bentley's death, Warburton spoke of him as "a truly great and injured man," &c.; before it, he invariably, though timidly, disparaged him. Swift never assailed Bentley after the *Tale of a Tub*. But Arbuthnot, another member of the Scriblerus Club, parodied Bentley's Horace and Phædrus in the *Miscellanies* of 1727; and published a supplement to *Gulliver's Travels*, describing "The State of Learning in the Empire of Lilliput." "Bullum is a tall, raw-boned man, I believe near six inches and a half high; from his infancy he applied himself with great industry to the old Blefuscudian language, in which he made such a progress that he almost forgot his native Lilliputian"—an unlucky stroke, seeing that Bentley's command of English was one of his marked gifts. This, however, is characteristic of all the satire directed against Bentley by the literary men who allowed a criticism of taste, but treated a criticism of texts as soulless pedantry. There is plenty of banter, but not one point. And the cause is plain—they understood nothing of Bentley's work. Take Pope's extended satire in the fourth *Dunciad*. It is merely a series of variations, as brilliant and as thin as Thalberg's setting of "Home, sweet home," on the simple theme, "Dull Bentley." A small satellite of Pope, one David Mallet, wrote a "Poem on Verbal Criticism," in which he greets Bentley as "great eldest-born of Dulness!" Mallet deserves to be remembered with Garth.

In June, 1742, having completed eighty years and some months, Bentley was still able to examine for the Craven University Scholarships—when Christopher Smart was one of the successful competitors. A few weeks later the end came. His grandson tells it thus: "He was seized with a complaint" (pleuritic fever, it was said) "that in his opinion seemed to indicate a necessity of immediate bleeding; Dr. Heberden, then a young physician practising in Cambridge, was of a contrary opinion, and the patient acquiesced." Bentley died on July 14, 1742. Dr. Wallis, of Stamford—an old friend and adviser who was summoned, but arrived too late—said that the measure suggested by the sufferer was that which he himself would have taken.

Bentley was buried in the chapel of Trinity College, on the north side of the communion-rails. The Latin oration

then customary was pronounced by Philip Yonge, afterwards Public Orator, and Bishop of Norwich. The day
of Bentley's funeral was that on which George Baker left
Eton for King's College—the eminent physician to whom
it was partly due that Cambridge became the University
of Porson. The small square stone in the pavement of
the College Chapel bears these words only:

H. S. E.

RICHARDUS BENTLEY S. T. P. R.

Obiit xiv. Jul. 1742.

Ætatis 80.

[Sanctae
Theologiae
Professor
Regius.]

The words *Magister Collegii* would naturally have been
added to the second line; but in the view of those Fellows who acknowledged the judgment of April, 1738, the
Mastership had since then been vacant. In the hall of the
College, where many celebrated names are commemorated
by the portraits on the walls, places of honour are assigned
to Bacon, Barrow, Newton, and Bentley. The features of
the great scholar speak with singular force from the can-
vas of Thornhill, who painted him in his forty-eighth year,
the very year in which his struggle with the College began. That picture, Bentley's own bequest, is in the Master's Lodge. The pose of the head is haughty, almost
defiant; the eyes, which are large, prominent, and full of
bold vivacity, have a light in them as if Bentley were
looking straight at an impostor whom he had detected,
but who still amused him; the nose, strong and slightly
tip-tilted, is moulded as if Nature had wished to show
what a nose can do for the combined expression of scorn
and sagacity; and the general effect of the countenance,
at a first glance, is one which suggests power—frank, self-
assured, sarcastic, and, I fear we must add, insolent: yet,

standing a little longer before the picture, we become
aware of an essential kindness in those eyes of which the
gaze is so direct and intrepid; we read in the whole face
a certain keen veracity; and the sense grows—this was a
man who could hit hard, but who would not strike a foul
blow, and whose ruling instinct, whether always a sure
guide or not, was to pierce through falsities to truth.

CHAPTER XIII.

IT will not be the object of these concluding pages to weigh Bentley's merits against those of any individual scholar in past or present times. The attempt, in such a case, to construct an order of merit amuses the competitive instinct of mankind, and may be an interesting exercise of private judgment, but presupposes a common measure for claims which are often, by their nature, incommensurable. A more useful task is to consider the nature of Bentley's place in that development of scholarship which extends from the fifteenth century to our own day. Caution may be needed to avoid drawing lines of a delusive sharpness between periods of which the characteristics rather melt into each other. The fact remains, however, that general tendencies were successively prevalent in a course which can be traced. And Bentley stands in a well-marked relation both to those who preceded and to those who followed him.

At his birth in 1662 rather more than two centuries had elapsed since the beginning of the movement which was to restore ancient literature to the modern world. During the earlier of these two centuries — from about 1450 to 1550 — the chief seat of the revival had been Italy, which thus retained by a new title that intellectual primacy of Europe which had seemed on the point of passing from the lands of the South. Latin literature engrossed the early Italian scholars, who regarded themselves as literary heirs of Rome, restored to their rights after ages of dispossession. The beauty of classical form came as a surprise and a delight to these children of the middle age; they admired and enjoyed; they could not criticise. The more rhetorical parts of silver Latinity pleased them best; a preference natural to the Italian genius. And meanwhile Greek studies had remained in the background. The purest and most perfect examples of form—those which Greek literature affords—were not present to the mind of the earlier Renaissance. Transalpine students resorted to Italy as for initiation into sacred mysteries. The highest eminence in classical scholarship was regarded as a birthright of Italians. The small circle of immortals which included Poggio and Politian admitted only one foreigner, Erasmus, whose cosmopolitan tone gave no wound to the national susceptibility of Italians, and whose conception, though larger than theirs, rested on the same basis. That basis was the *imitatio veterum*, the literary reproduction of ancient form. Erasmus was nearer than any of his predecessors or contemporaries to the idea of a critical philology. His natural gifts for it are sufficiently manifest. But his want of critical method, and of the sense which requires it, appears in his edition of the Greek Testament.

In the second half of the sixteenth century a new period is opened by a Frenchman of Italian origin, Joseph Scaliger. Hitherto scholarship had been busy with the form of classical literature. The new effort is to comprehend the matter. By his Latin compositions and translations Scaliger is connected with the Italian age of Latin stylists.

But his most serious and characteristic work was the endeavour to frame a critical chronology of the ancient world. He was peculiarly well-fitted to effect a transition from the old to the new aim, because his industry could not be reproached with dulness. "People had thought that æsthetic pleasure could be purchased only at the cost of criticism," says Bernays; "now they saw the critical workshop itself lit up with the glow of artistic inspiration." A different praise belongs to Scaliger's great and indefatigable contemporary, Isaac Casaubon. His groans over Athenæus, which sometimes reverberate in the brilliant and faithful pages of Mr. Pattison, appear to warrant Casaubon's comparison of his toils to the labours of penal servitude ("*catenati in ergastulo labores*"). Bernhardy defines the merit of Casaubon as that of having been the first to popularise a connected knowledge of ancient life and manners. Two things had now been done. The charm of Latin style had been appreciated. The contents of ancient literature, both Latin and Greek, had been surveyed, and partly registered.

Bentley approached ancient literature on the side which had been chiefly cultivated in the age nearest to his own. When we first find him at work, under Stillingfleet's roof, or in the libraries of Oxford, he is evidently less occupied with the form than with the matter. He reads extensively, making indexes for his own use; he seeks to possess the contents of the classical authors, whether already printed or accessible only in manuscript. An incident told by Cumberland is suggestive. Bentley was talking one day with his favourite daughter, when she hinted a regret that he had devoted so much of his time to criticism, rather than to original composition. He acknowledged the justice of the remark. "But the wit and genius of those old heathens," he said, "beguiled me: and as I despaired of raising myself up to their standard upon fair ground, I thought the only chance I had of looking over their heads was to get upon their shoulders." These are the words of a man who had turned to ancient literature in the spirit of Scaliger rather than in that of the Italian Latinists.

But in the Letter to Mill—when Bentley was only twenty-eight—we perceive that his wide reading had already made him alive to the necessity of a work which no previous scholar had thoroughly or successfully undertaken. This work was the purification of the classical texts. They were still deformed by a mass of errors which could not even be detected without the aid of accurate knowledge, grammatical and metrical. The great scholars before Bentley, with all their admirable merits, had in this respect resembled aeronauts, gazing down on a beautiful and varied country, in which, however, the pedestrian is liable to be stopped by broken bridges or quaking swamps. These difficulties of the ground, to which Bentley's patient march had brought him, engaged his *first* care. No care could hope to be successful—this he saw clearly—unless armed with the resources which previous scholarship had provided. The critic of a text should command the stylist's tact in language, and also the knowledge of the commentator. In the Latin preface to his edition of Horace, Bentley explains that his work is to be textual, illustrative; and then proceeds:

"All honour to the learned men who have expatiated in the field of commentary. They have done a most valuable work, which would now have to be done from the beginning, if they had not been beforehand; a work without which my reader cannot hope to pass the threshold of these present labours. That wide reading and erudi-

10

tion, that knowledge of all Greek and Latin antiquity, in which the commentaries have their very essence, are merely subordinate aids to textual criticism. A man should have all that at his fingers' ends, before he can venture, without insane rashness, to pass criticism on any ancient author. But, besides this, there is need of the keenest judgment, of sagacity and quickness, of a certain divining tact and inspiration (*divinandi quadam peritia et* μαντικῇ), as was said of Aristarchus—a faculty which can be acquired by no constancy of toil or length of life, but comes solely by the gift of nature and the happy star."

Let it be noted that Bentley's view is relative to his own day. It is because such men as Casaubon have gone before that he can thus define his own purpose. Learning, inspired by insight, is now to be directed to the attainment of textual accuracy. Bentley's distinction is not so much the degree of his insight—rare as this was—but rather his method of applying it. It might be said: Bentley turned the course of scholarship aside from grander objects, philosophical, historical, literary, and forced it into a narrow verbal groove. If Bentley's criticism had been verbal only—which it was not—such an objection would still be unjust. We in these days are accustomed to Greek and Latin texts which, though they may be still more or less unsound, are seldom so unsound as largely to obscure the author's meaning, or seriously to mar our enjoyment of his work as a work of art. But for this state of things we have mainly to thank the impulse given by Bentley.

In Bentley's time very many Latin authors, and nearly all Greek authors, were known only through texts teeming with every fault that could spring from a scribe's ignorance of grammar, metre, and sense. Suppose a piece of very bad English handwriting, full of erasures and corrections, sent to be printed at a foreign press. The for-

eign printer's first proof would be likely to contain some
flagrant errors which a very slight acquaintance with our
language would suffice to amend, and also many other
errors which an Englishman could correct with more or
less confidence, but in which a foreign corrector of the
press would not even perceive anything amiss. In 1700
most of the classical texts, especially Greek, were very
much what such a proof-sheet would be if only those flagrant errors had been removed which a very imperfect
knowledge of English would reveal. Relatively to his contemporaries, Bentley might be compared with the Englishman of our supposed case, and his predecessors with the
foreign correctors of the press.

Space fails for examples, but I may give one. An epi-
gram of Callimachus begins thus:

> τὴν ἁλίην Εὔδημος, ἐφ' ἧς ἅλα λιτὸν ἐπελθὼν
> χειμῶνας μεγάλους ἐξέφυγεν δανέων,
> θῆκε θεοῖς Σαμόθραξι.

This had been taken to mean: "Eudemus dedicated
to the Samothracian gods that ship on which, after cross-
ing a smooth sea, he escaped from great storms [reading
Δαναῶν] of the Danai;" i. e., such storms as Æneas and
his companions suffered; or perhaps, storms off the coast
of the Troad. Bentley changed one letter (λ to σ, giving
ἐπέσθων), and showed the true meaning: "Eudemus dedicated to the Samothracian gods that salt-cellar from which
he ate frugal salt until he had escaped from the troublous
waves of usury." Eudemus was not an adventurous mar-
iner, but an impecunious person who had literally adopted
the advice of the Greek sage—"Borrow from thyself by
reducing thy diet"—and had gradually extricated himself
from debt by living on bread and salt.

The pleader for large views of antiquity, who is inclined to depreciate the humbler tasks of verbal criticism,
will allow that the frequency of such misapprehensions
was calculated to confuse.   It was not always, indeed,
that Bentley drew the veil aside with so light a touch;
but he has a reason to give.   "I would have you remember, it is immeasurably more difficult to make emendations at this day (in 1711) than it was in former years.
Those points which a mere collation of the manuscripts
flashed or forced upon the mind have generally been
seized and appropriated; and there is hardly anything
left, save what is to be extracted, by insight alone, from
the essence of the thought and the temper of the style.
Hence, in my recension of Horace, I give more things on
conjecture than through the help of manuscripts; and
unless I am wholly deceived, conjecture has usually been
the safer guide.   Where readings vary, the very repute of
the manuscript often misleads, and provokes the desire of
change.   But if a man is tempted to propose conjectures
against the witness of all the manuscripts, Fear and Shame
pluck him by the ear; his sole guides are reason—the
light from the author's thoughts, and their constraining
power.   Suppose that one or two manuscripts furnish a
reading which others discountenance.   It is in vain that
you demand belief for your one or two witnesses against
a multitude, unless you bring as many arguments as would
almost suffice to prove the point of themselves, without
any manuscript testimony at all.   Shake off, then, the
exclusive reverence for scribes.   Dare to have a mind of
your own.   Gauge each reading by the mould of the
writer's expression and the stamp of his style; then, and
not sooner, pronounce your verdict."

No school of textual criticism, however conservative, has

denied that conjecture is sometimes our sole resource.
Bentley differs from the principles of more recent criticism
chiefly in recognising less distinctly that conjecture should
be the *last* resource. Great as was his tact in the use of
manuscripts, he had, as a rule, too little of that respect for
diplomatic evidence which appears, for instance, in Ritschl's
remark that almost any manuscript will sometimes, however rarely, deserve more belief than we can give even to a
conjecture which is intrinsically probable. The contrast,
here, between Bentley's procedure and that of Casaubon—
whose caution is often more in the spirit of modern textual science—may be illustrated by one example. Some
verses of the poet Ion stood thus in the texts of the geog-
rapher Strabo:

$$\text{Εὐβοΐδα μὲν γῆν λεπτὸς Εὐρίπου κλύδων}$$
$$\text{Βοιωτίας ἐχώρισ' ἀκτῆς, ἐκτέμνων}$$
$$\text{πρὸς Κρῆτα πορθμόν.}$$

When Casaubon had made the necessary change ἐκτεμών,
he held his hand. "I can point out," said Casaubon, "that
this place is corrupt; amend it I cannot, *without the help
of manuscripts.*" Not so Bentley: he confidently gives
us, ἀκτὴν ἐκτεμὼν | προβλῆτα πορθμῷ. Now, if Casaubon
was ineffectual, Bentley was precipitate. Nothing, surely,
was needed but to shift Βοιωτίας from the beginning to the
end of its verse. If we suppose that the words πρὸς Κρῆτα
πορθμόν belonged to what precedes, and not (as is quite
possible) to something now lost which followed, then we
get a clear sense, expressed in a thoroughly classical form.
"The narrow waters of the Euripus have parted Euboea
from the Boeotian shore, so shaping it (ἐκτεμών), that it
looks toward the Cretan sea;" *i. e.*, the island of Euboea
runs out in a S. E. S. direction. Ancient writers often de-

note *aspect* by naming a region, though distant and invisible, towards which a land looks. Thus Herodotus describes a part of the north Sicilian coast as that which " looks towards Tyrrhenia " (πρὸς Τυρσηνίην τετραμμένη). Milton imitates this device:

> " Where the great vision of the guarded Mount
> Looks towards Namancos and Bayona's hold."

I never understood how Milton came to write those lines till I thought of seeking a clue in Camden (of whom there is another trace in *Lycidas*); and he gave it. Speaking of the Cornish coast adjacent to St. Michael's Mount, Camden remarks, "there is no other place in this island that looks towards Spain." This fact was present to Milton's mind, and he wished to work it in; then he consulted Mercator's Atlas, where he found the town of Namancos marked near Cape Finisterre, and the Castle of Bayona also prominent; these gave him his ornate periphrasis for " Spain."

Though Bentley had little poetical taste, it was in poetry that he exercised his faculty of emendation, not only with most zest, but with most success. The reason is simple. Metre enabled Bentley to show a knowledge in which no predecessor had equalled him; it also supplied a framework which limited his rashness. In prose, his temerity was sometimes wanton. We have seen (chapter x.) how his *illa* would have swept *Itala* from the text of Augustine. One other instance may be given. Seneca compares a man who cannot keep his temper to one who cannot control his limbs. " Ægros scimus nervos esse, cum invitis nobis moventur. Senex aut infirmi corporis est, qui, cum ambulare vult, *currit*." " We know that something is wrong with our nerves, when they act against our will.

It is only an old man, or an invalid, who, when he means
to walk, *runs*." By "*currit*," Seneca describes a well-
known symptom of degeneration in the nervous system,
which modern medical science terms "festination."
"Now," says Bentley, "I do not see how this feeble person can show such agility. Clearly *currit* should be *cor-
ruit*. He tries to walk—and *tumbles down*. Bentley did
not observe that the sentence just before proves "currit"
to be right: "Speed is not to be desired," says Seneca,
"unless it can be checked at our pleasure, . . . and reduced
from a run to a walk" (a *cursu* ad gradum reduci). Of
previous scholars, the best skilled in metre was Scaliger.
Yet Scaliger's acquaintance with the metres of the *classical*
age was by no means accurate; thus his anapæsts have
the same fault as those of Buchanan and Grotius; and the
iambic verses which he prefixed to his work *De Emenda-
tione Temporum* have two metrical mistakes in four lines.
While invariably mentioning Casaubon with the respect
due to so great a name, Bentley has more than once occasion to indicate the false quantities which his conjectures
involve. Thus a line of Sophocles, as given by Suidas,
begins with the words πέπλους ("robes") τενίσαι. What
is τενίσαι? Casaubon—followed by Meursius and by Gat-
aker (one of the best English Hellenists before Bentley)—
proposed κτενίσαι, "to comb" or "card." Pointing out
that this will not do, since the second syllable must be
long, Bentley restores πέπλους τε νῆσαι, "and to weave
robes."

As a commentator, he deals chiefly, though not exclusively, with points of grammar or metre bearing on
the criticism of the text. Here he has two merits, each
in a high degree: he instructs and suggests. The notes
on Horace and Manilius, for example, constantly fail to

persuade, but seldom fail to teach. It is to be wished
that Bentley had written commentary, not merely in support of emendations, but continuously illustrating the language and matter of classical authors. If such a commentary had been added to his critical notes on Aristophanes, the whole must have been a great work. His
power in *general* commentary is best seen in his treatment of particular points raised by his argument on the
Letters of Phalaris. Take, for instance, his remarks on
the Sophist's use of πρόνοια to mean "divine Providence,"
and of στοιχεῖον as "a natural element;" where he shows
that, before Plato, the former was used only of human
forecast, and the latter to denote a letter of the alphabet:
or, again, his remark on such phrases as λέγεται, "it is
said"—that Greek writers commonly use such phrases,
not to intimate doubt, but, on the contrary, where the
literary witnesses are more numerous than can convenient-
ly be enumerated. Other comments are of yet larger
scope. Thus, speaking of the fact that most ecclesiastical
writers place the date of Pythagoras too low, he notices
the need of allowing for a general disturbing cause—the
tendency to represent Greek antiquity as more recent than
Jewish. Answering the objection that a Greek comedy
would not have admitted a glaring anachronism, Bentley
reminds Boyle that, in one of these comedies, Hercules
comes on the scene with his private tutor, who gives him
his choice of several standard works, including Homer;
but the young hero chooses a treatise on cookery which
was popular in the dramatist's time. Some of Bentley's
happiest comments of this kind occur in his reply to Anthony Collins, who in his "Discourse of Free-thinking"
had appealed to the most eminent of the ancients. Here,
for instance, is a remark on Cicero's philosophical dia-

logues. "In all the disputes he introduces between the various sects, after the speeches are ended, every man sticks where he was before; not one convert is made (as is common in modern dialogue), nor brought over in the smallest article. For he avoided that violation of decorum; he had observed, in common life, that all persevered in their sects, and maintained every nostrum without reserve."

Bentley's "higher criticism"—of ancient history, chronology, philosophy, literature—is mainly represented by the dissertation on Phalaris; but his calibre can also be estimated by his sketchy treatment of particular topics in the reply to Collins and in the Boyle Lectures. Of the scholars before Bentley, Usher and Selden might be partly compared with him in this province; but the only one, perhaps, who had built similar work on a comparable basis of classical learning was Scaliger. In Bentley's estimation, to judge by the tone of his references to Scaliger, no one stood higher. With all the differences between Bentley and Scaliger, there was this essential resemblance, that both men vivified great masses of learning by ardent, though dissimilar, genius:

"Spiritus intus alit, totamque infusa per artus
Mens agitat molem, et magno se in corpore miscet."

While Scaliger had constantly before him the conception of antiquity as a whole to be mentally grasped, Bentley's criticism rested on a knowledge more complete in detail; it was also conducted with a closer and more powerful logic. The fact which has told most against the popular diffusion of Bentley's fame is that he is so much greater than any one of his books. Probably many school-boys have passed through a stage of secretly wondering why

10*

so much was thought of this Bentley, known to them only
as the proposer of some rash emendations on Horace.
Bentley's true greatness is not easily understood until
his work has been surveyed in its entirety, with a clear
sense of the time at which it was done; until the original
learning and native power of his method are appreciated
apart from the sometimes brilliant, sometimes faulty result; until, in short, the letter of his record is lit up for
us by the living force of his character and mind.

What has been the nature of Bentley's influence on the
subsequent course of scholarship? In the first place, it
cannot be properly said that he founded a school. That
phrase may express the relation of disciples to the master
who has personally formed them, as Ruhnken belongs to
the school of Hemsterhuys; or, where there has been no
personal intercourse, it may denote the tradition of a well-
defined scope or style; as the late Richard Shilleto (in his
masterly edition of Demosthenes "On the Embassy," for
instance) belongs to the school of Porson. Wolf said that
if Cambridge had required Bentley to lecture on classics,
he would probably have left a more distinct impress on
some of those who came after him. Though the tone of
Wolf's remark is more German than English, it applies
with peculiar point to Bentley, in whom the scholar was
before all things the man, and who often writes like one
who would have preferred to speak. But neither thus, nor
by set models of literary achievement, did Bentley create
anything so definite—or so narrow—as a school. Goethe
used the word "daemonic" to describe a power of mind
over mind which eludes natural analysis, but seems to involve a peculiar union of keen insight with moral self-reli-
ance. In the sphere of scholarship, the influence which
Bentley's spirit has exerted through his writings might be

called a great "daemonic" energy, a force which cannot be measured—like that, for instance, of Porson—by the positive effect of particular discoveries; a force which operates not only by the written letter, but also, and more widely still, by suggestion, stimulus, inspiration, almost as vivid as could be communicated by the voice, the countenance, the apprehended nature of a present teacher.

Bentley's influence has flowed in two main streams—the historical and literary criticism of classical antiquity, as best seen in the dissertation on Phalaris; the verbal criticism, as seen in his work on classical texts. Holland, and then Germany, received both currents. Wolf's inquiry into the origin of the Homeric poems, Niebuhr's examination of Roman legends, are the efforts of a criticism to which Bentley's dissertation on Phalaris gave the first pattern of method. On the other hand, Hermann's estimate of Bentley's Terence is one of the earlier testimonies to the effect which Bentley's verbal criticism had exercised; and Professor Nettleship has told us that the late Maurice Haupt, in his lectures at Berlin on the Epistles of Horace, ranked Bentley second to no other scholar. We, Bentley's countrymen, have felt his influence chiefly in the way of textual criticism. The historical and literary criticism by which he stimulated such men as Wolf was comparatively unappreciated in England until its effects returned upon this country from Germany. Bunsen could justly say, "Historical philology is the discovery of Bentley—the heritage and glory of German learning." At Cambridge, Bentley's home—where Markland, Wasse, and John Taylor had known him personally—it was natural that the contemporary view of his merits should be coloured by his own estimate; and he considered verbal emendation as his own forte. This opinion prevailed in the Cambridge tradition, which from Markland and Taylor passed into the school of Porson. It was in vain that Richard Dawes disparaged Bentley's textual criticism. Warburton and Lowth were more successful in prejudicing English opinion against other aspects of his work. That his labours on the Greek Testament were so little known in England from his death to Lachmann's time, is chiefly due to the fact (noticed by Tregelles) that Bishop Marsh, in translating Michaelis, omitted the passage relating to Bentley. But while English recognition was thus limited, Holland honoured him by the mouths of Ruhnken and Valckenaer. And the memoir of Bentley by F. A. Wolf may be regarded as registering an estimate which Germany has not essentially altered.

The place of Bentley in literature primarily depends on the fact that he represents England among a few great scholars, of various countries, who helped to restore classical learning in Europe. Nor is he merely one among them; he is one with whom an epoch begins. Erasmus marks the highest point reached in the sixteenth century by the genial study of antiquity on its literary side. Scaliger expresses the effort, at once erudite and artistic, to comprehend antiquity as a whole in the light of verified history. Casaubon embodies the devoted endeavour to comprehend ancient society in the light of its recorded manners, without irradiating or disturbing the effect by any play of personal thought or feeling. With Bentley that large conception of antiquity on the "real" side is still present, but as a condition tacitly presupposed, not as the evident guide of his immediate task. He feels the greatness of his predecessors as it could be felt only by their peer, but sees that the very foundations on which they built—the classical books themselves—must be rendered sound, if the edifice is to be upheld or completed. He does not disparage that "higher" criticism in which his own powers were so signally proved; rather his object is to establish it firmly on the only basis which can securely support it, the basis of ascertained texts. His labours were fruitful both in Greek and in Latin. However we may estimate his felicity in the two languages respectively, it cannot be said that he gave to either a clear preference over the other.

This is distinctive of his position relatively to the general course of subsequent scholarship. During the latter part of the eighteenth century several causes conspired to fix attention upon Greek. The elastic freedom of the Greek language and literature, of Greek action and art, was congenial to the spirit of that time, insurgent as it was against traditional authority, and impatient to find a reasonable order of life by a return to nature. Wolf, in 1795, touched a chord which vibrated throughout Europe when he claimed the Iliad and the Odyssey as groups of songs which in a primitive age had spoken directly to the hearts of the people. His theory, raising a host of special questions, stimulated research in the whole range of that matchless literature which begins with Homer. The field of Greek studies, as compared with Latin, was still comparatively fresh. Latin had long been familiar as the language which scholars wrote, or even spoke; and the further progress of Latin learning was delayed by the belief that there was little more to learn. Greek, on the other hand, attracted acute minds not only by its intrinsic charm, but by the hope of discovery; the Greek scholar, like the Greek sailor of old, was attended by visions of treasures that might await him in the region of the sunset.

Porson was born in 1759 and died in 1808. In his lifetime, and for more than a generation after his death, scholars were principally occupied with Greek. Amongst many eminent names, it would be enough to mention Wyttenbach, Brunck, Hermann, Boeckh, Lobeck, Bekker, Elmsley, Dobree, Blomfield, Gaisford, Thirlwall. In Latin scholarship, Heyne's Virgil was perhaps the most considerable performance of Porson's day. Then Niebuhr arose, and turned new currents of interest towards Rome. His examination of early Roman tradition did much the same work for Latin which Wolf's Homeric theory had done for Greek. Ideas of startling novelty stimulated the critical study of a whole literature; and the value of the impulse was independent of the extent to which the ideas themselves were sound. Niebuhr's thoughts, like Wolf's, were given to the world in a propitious hour. Wolf broached views welcome to the mind of the Revolution; Niebuhr proposed a complex problem of fascinating interest at a moment when intellectual pursuits were resumed with a new zest after the exhaustion of the Napoleonic wars. And then, at no long interval, came the works which may be regarded as fundamental in the recent Latin philology—those of Lachmann, Ritschl, Mommsen.

Bentley's name is the last of first-rate magnitude which occurs above the point at which Greek and Latin studies begin to diverge. His critical method, his pregnant ideas have influenced the leaders of progress in both fields. Wolf's memoir of Bentley has been mentioned. Niebuhr also speaks of him as towering like a giant amidst a generation of dwarfs. His genius was recognised by Ritschl as by Porson. It is still possible to ask, Was Bentley stronger in Greek or in Latin? I have heard a very eminent scholar say—in Latin: the general voice would probably say—in Greek; and this is hardly disputable, if our

test is to be success in textual criticism. Bentley has
given few, if any, Latin emendations so good as his best
on Aristophanes, Callimachus, Nicander, and some other
Greek authors. Yet the statement needs to be guarded
and explained. In Bentley's time, Latin studies were more
advanced than Greek. Bentley's emendations, as a general rule, are best when the text is worst. The Greek
texts, in which the first harvest had not yet been reaped,
offered him a better field than the Latin. His personal
genius, with its vivacity somewhat impatient of formula,
was also more Greek than Latin; his treatment of Greek
usually seems more sympathetic; but it might be doubted
whether his positive knowledge of the Latin language and
literature was inferior. If it is said that there are flaws
in his Latin prose, it may be replied that we have none of
his Greek prose.

The gain of scholarship during the last fifty years has
been chiefly in three provinces — study of manuscripts,
study of inscriptions, and comparative philology. The
direct importance of archæology for classical learning has
of late years been winning fuller recognition—to the advantage of both. In Bentley's time no one of these four
studies had yet become scientific. That very fact best
illustrates the calibre of the man who, a century and a
half ago, put forth principles of textual criticism afterwards adopted by Lachmann; merited the title, "first of
critics," from such an editor of Greek inscriptions as
Boeckh; divined the presence of the digamma in the
text of Homer; treated an obscure branch of numis-
matics with an insight which the most recent researches,
aided by new resources, recognise as extraordinary. Bentley's qualities, mental and moral, fitted him to be a pioneer over a wide region, rather than, like Porson, the per-

fect cultivator of a limited domain; Bentley cleared new
ground, made new paths, opened new perspectives, ranged
through the length and breadth of ancient literature as
Hercules, in the *Trachiniae* of Sophocles, claims to have
roamed through Hellas, sweeping from hill, lake, and for-
est those monstrous forms before which superstition had
quailed, or which helpless apathy had suffered to infest
the dark places of the land.

Probably the study of classical antiquity, in the largest
sense, has never been more really vigorous than it is at
the present day. If so, it is partly because that study
relies no longer upon a narrow or exclusive prescription,
but upon a reasonable perception of its proper place
amongst the studies which belong to a liberal education;
and because the diffusion of that which is specially named
science has at the same time spread abroad the only spirit
in which any kind of knowledge can be prosecuted to a
result of lasting intellectual value. Whilst every year
tends to refine the subdivision of labour in that vast field,
Bentley's work teaches a simple lesson which is still applicable to every part of it. The literary activity of the
present day has multiplied attractive facilities for becoming acquainted with the ancient classics at second-hand.
Every sensible person will rejoice that such facilities exist; they are excellent in their own way. Only it is important not to forget the difference between the knowledge at second-hand and the knowledge at first-hand,
whether regard is had to the educational effect of the
process, or to the worth of the acquisition, or to the
hope of further advance. Even with a Bentley's power,
a Bentley could have been made only by his method—
by his devoted and systematic study, not of books about
the classics, but of the classical texts themselves; by test-

ing, at each step, his comprehension of what he read; by not allowing the mere authority of tradition to supersede the free exercise of independent judgment; and by always remembering that the very right of such judgment to independence must rest on the patience, the intelligence, the completeness with which the tradition itself has been surveyed.

THE END.

ENGLISH MEN OF LETTERS.

EDITED BY JOHN MORLEY.

The following volumes are now ready:

JOHNSON..LESLIE STEPHEN.
GIBBON..J. C. MORISON.
SCOTT..R. H. HUTTON.
SHELLEY..J. A. SYMONDS.
HUME...Professor HUXLEY.
GOLDSMITH..WILLIAM BLACK.
DEFOE..WILLIAM MINTO.
BURNS..Principal SHAIRP.
SPENSER..The DEAN OF ST. PAUL'S.
THACKERAY..ANTHONY TROLLOPE.
BURKE..JOHN MORLEY.
MILTON...MARK PATTISON.
SOUTHEY..Professor DOWDEN.
CHAUCER..Professor A. W. WARD.
BUNYAN...J. A. FROUDE.
COWPER...GOLDWIN SMITH.
POPE...LESLIE STEPHEN.
BYRON..JOHN NICHOL.
LOCKE..THOMAS FOWLER.
WORDSWORTH...F. MYERS.
DRYDEN...G. SAINTSBURY.
LANDOR...Professor SIDNEY COLVIN.
DE QUINCEY...Professor D. MASSON.
LAMB...The Rev. ALFRED AINGER.
BENTLEY..Professor JEBB.

12mo, Cloth, 75 cents per volume.

HAWTHORNE. By HENRY JAMES, Jr..................12mo, Cloth, $1 00.

VOLUMES IN PREPARATION:

SWIFT..JOHN MORLEY.
GRAY...JOHN MORLEY.
ADAM SMITH...LEONARD H. COURTNEY.
DICKENS..Professor A. W. WARD.

Others will be announced.

PUBLISHED BY HARPER & BROTHERS, NEW YORK.

☞ HARPER & BROTHERS *will send any of the above works by mail, postage prepaid, to any part of the United States, on receipt of the price.*

BY CHARLES LAMB.

THE WORKS OF CHARLES LAMB. Comprising his Letters, Poems, Essays of Elia, Essays upon Shakespeare, Hogarth, &c., and a Sketch of his Life, with the Final Memorials, by T. NOON TALFOURD. Portrait. 2 vols., 12mo, Cloth, $3 00.

His works will be received as among the most elaborately finished gems of literature ; as cabinet specimens which express the utmost delicacy, purity, and tenderness of the national intellect, together with the rarest felicity of finish and expression.—DE QUINCEY.

The glimpses and flashes which Charles Lamb flings over a subject show us more of its bearings than a hundred farthing candles held up by the hands of formal and pragmatical literati. Everything that rises up before his mind is set before us in vivid beauty. The style of his prose is exceedingly beautiful, in imitation of those rich elder writers of ours, but always easy, simple, graceful, and concise.—*Blackwood's Magazine.*

TALES FROM SHAKESPEARE. In 2 vols. Vol. I. Comedies. Vol. II. Tragedies. By CHARLES and MARY LAMB. 32mo, Paper, 25 cents each.

These tales form one of the most useful and agreeable companions to the understanding of Shakespeare that have ever been produced.—*New York Evening Mail.*

These pleasant little hand-books should be the constant companions of Shakespearian students.—*Christian Advocate,* New York.

ADVENTURES OF ULYSSES. By CHARLES LAMB. 32mo, Paper, 25 cents.

Published by HARPER & BROTHERS, New York.

☞ *Any of the above works sent by mail, postage prepaid, to any part of the United States, on receipt of the price.*

THE LIFE

OF

JOHN LOCKE.

BY

H. R. FOX BOURNE.

2 vols., 8vo, Cloth, $5 00.

The biographer of Locke has interwoven the private and public events of the period skilfully together, so that we see Locke not as an abstract philosopher, but as the child of his age, who was to a large degree the outcome of a period which, nevertheless, he powerfully helped to mould. He has given us a work which supplies an unmistakable want in the literature of English philosophy, and which will make the thoroughly English features of the philosopher familiar to the present generation. He has shown us Locke in connection with his time, and has traced the various ways in which he exercised healthful influence upon it, and became the source of similar influence to succeeding generations. We cordially welcome this excellent piece of biography, and we have little doubt that it will become a standard work.—*British Quarterly Review*, London.

Mr. Fox Bourne has added considerably to our knowledge of the details of Locke's life. We have now a complete picture of the man and his surroundings.—*Examiner*, London.

To revive the memory of such a man is obviously an undertaking of much moment, and Mr. Fox Bourne has felt the responsibility of his task. He spares no pains; his life of Locke evinces much editorial care, and contains novel information.—*Athenæum*, London.

Mr. Fox Bourne is able to state most justly in his Preface that more than half of the contents of this work is derived from hitherto unused manuscripts, and that by them, apart from their independent worth, altogether new light is thrown on most of the information that is not actually new. * * * A conscientious and painstaking performance, and will well repay a careful reading.—*Academy*, London.

It is clear and interesting to read, and will be of permanent value to students of Locke's work and times.—*Saturday Review*, London.

PUBLISHED BY HARPER & BROTHERS, NEW YORK.

☞ HARPER & BROTHERS *will send the above work by mail, postage prepaid, to any part of the United States, on receipt of the price.*

W. M. THACKERAY'S WORKS.

HARPER'S HOUSEHOLD EDITION.

12mo, Cloth.

NOVELS: Vanity Fair.— Pendennis.— The Newcomes.— The Virginians.—Adventures of Philip.—Esmond, and Lovel the Widower. Illustrated. Six volumes, $1 50 per volume.

MISCELLANEOUS WRITINGS: Barry Lyndon, Hoggarty Diamond, &c.—Paris and Irish Sketch Books, &c.—Book of Snobs, Sketches, &c.—Four Georges, English Humorists, Roundabout Papers, &c.—Catherine, Christmas Books, &c. Illustrated. Five Volumes. $1 50 per volume.

HARPER'S POPULAR EDITION.

8vo, Paper.

	CENTS
Vanity Fair ....Ill'd.......	80
Pendennis............................Ill'd........	75
The Newcomes......................Ill'd........	90
The Virginians.....................Ill'd........	90
The Adventures of Philip.............Ill'd.......	60
Henry Esmond, and Lovel the Widower..Ill'd.......	60
The Great Hoggarty Diamond	20
Denis Duval.........................Ill'd.......	25

PUBLISHED BY HARPER & BROTHERS, NEW YORK.

☞ HARPER & BROTHERS *will send any of the above volumes by mail, postage prepaid, to any part of the United States or Canada, on receipt of the price.*

MOTLEY'S HISTORIES.

CHEAP EDITION.

THE RISE OF THE DUTCH REPUBLIC. A History. By JOHN
LOTHROP MOTLEY, LL.D., D.C.L. With a Portrait of William of
Orange. 3 volumes, 8vo, Cloth with Paper Labels, Uncut Edges
and Gilt Tops, $6 00. *Sold only in Sets.*

HISTORY OF THE UNITED NETHERLANDS: from the Death
of William the Silent to the Twelve-Years' Truce. With a full
View of the English-Dutch Struggle against Spain, and of the
Origin and Destruction of the Spanish Armada. By JOHN
LOTHROP MOTLEY, LL.D., D.C.L. With Portraits. 4 volumes,
8vo, Cloth with Paper Labels, Uncut Edges and Gilt Tops, $8 00.
Sold only in Sets.

LIFE AND DEATH OF JOHN OF BARNEVELD, Advocate of
Holland. With a View of the Primary Causes and Movements
of the "Thirty-Years' War." By JOHN LOTHROP MOTLEY, LL.D.,
D.C.L. Illustrated. 2 volumes, 8vo, Cloth with Paper Labels,
Uncut Edges and Gilt Tops, $4 00. *Sold only in Sets.*

This edition of Motley's "Complete Historical Works" affords an opportunity to the collector of choice standard works to fill a possible vacancy in
his library at a moderate cost. The reader of Motley always returns to the
perusal of his writings with a zest which may be compared to the taste of
the ripe strawberries in early June. The freshness of his mind never fails
to give a flavor to his narrative. His descriptions read less like a recital of
the faded past than a vivid picture of living scenes. No historian transports
so much of himself into his writings; and though without the faintest trace
of egotism, they are always intensely human and individual.—*N.Y. Tribune.*

The original Library Edition, on larger paper, of Mr. Motley's
Histories can still be supplied: "The Dutch Republic," 3 vols.;
"The History of the United Netherlands," 4 vols.; "Life and Death
of John of Barneveld," 2 vols. Price *per volume*, in Cloth, $3 50;
in Sheep, $4 00; in Half Calf or Half Morocco, $5 75. *The volumes
of this original edition sold separately.*

Published by HARPER & BROTHERS, New York.

☞ *Sent by mail, postage prepaid, to any part of the United States,
on receipt of the price.*

By GEORGE WILLIAM CURTIS.

LOTUS - EATING. A Summer Book. Illustrated from Designs
by Kensett. 12mo, Cloth, $1 50.

This delightful volume is a record of summer rambles, touching gracefully
on many of the most interesting spots in American scenery, and giving a
series of lively pictures of the celebrated places of fashionable resort.

PRUE AND I. 12mo, Cloth, $1 50.

In the character and fancies of an old book-keeper, the author of these
charming essays has embodied the sweetest and most genial humor which
has graced English literature since the delightful Essays of Elia.

NILE NOTES OF A HOWADJI. 12mo, Cloth, $1 50.

The author takes the reader with him into rare and beautiful scenes of
nature, unfolds the mysteries of Arabian life, and reproduces the strange
incidents of a unique tour in language of wonderful vividness and force.

THE HOWADJI IN SYRIA. 12mo, Cloth, $1 50.

It abounds in picturesque descriptions of the marvels of the Holy Land,
throwing fresh light on ancient localities, and imbued with the spirit of
sympathy and reverence for the sacred scenes which it calls forth from the
dim oblivion of the past.

THE POTIPHAR PAPERS. Illustrated by Drawings from
Hoppin. 12mo, Cloth, $1 50.

As graphic and telling descriptions of a peculiar phase of American society, they are unexcelled; the fresh and sparkling wit, the genial humor,
and keen and truthful satire with which "Our Best Society" is dissected,
have delighted thousands, and made "Mrs. Potiphar" a proverb.

TRUMPS. A Novel. Illustrated by Hoppin. 12mo, Cloth,
$2 00.

Gay and sparkling in its external aspect, the novel is evidently the fruit
of profound insight and conscientious adherence to the truth of nature, as
well as of acute observation and a spontaneous liveliness of humor. The
materials are drawn from the many-colored exhibitions of fashionable and
commercial life in New York; and they are wrought up into a cabinet of
portraitures which vividly reflect the familiar traits of the original.

Published by HARPER & BROTHERS, New York.

☞ *Any of the above works sent by mail, postage prepaid, to any part of
the United States, on receipt of the price.*

Date Due

Dec 3 '33			
Dec 13 '33			
Dec 2 '54			